the
great
office
detox

By the same author

De-Junk Your Mind

Dawna Walter

the
great
office
detox

minimize stress and
maximize job satisfaction

MICHAEL JOSEPH
an imprint of
PENGUIN BOOKS

MICHAEL JOSEPH

Published by the Penguin Group
Penguin Books Ltd, 80 Strand, London WC2R 0RL, England
Penguin Group (USA) Inc., 375 Hudson Street, New York, New York 10014, USA
Penguin Group (Canada), 90 Eglinton Avenue East, Suite 700, Toronto, Ontario, Canada M4P 2Y3
(a division of Pearson Penguin Canada Inc.)
Penguin Ireland, 25 St Stephen's Green, Dublin 2, Ireland (a division of Penguin Books Ltd)
Penguin Group (Australia), 250 Camberwell Road,
Camberwell, Victoria 3124, Australia (a division of Pearson Australia Group Pty Ltd)
Penguin Books India Pvt Ltd, 11 Community Centre,
Panchsheel Park, New Delhi – 110 017, India
Penguin Group (NZ), 67 Apollo Drive, Mairangi Bay,
Auckland 1310, New Zealand (a division of Pearson New Zealand Ltd)
Penguin Books (South Africa) (Pty) Ltd, 24 Sturdee Avenue,
Rosebank, Johannesburg 2196, South Africa

Penguin Books Ltd, Registered Offices: 80 Strand, London WC2R 0RL, England

www.penguin.com

First published 2007
1

Grateful acknowledgement is made for permission to use the Home Desk, designed by
Bruno Fattorini for MDF Italia, supplied by Viaduct, 1–10 Summers Street, London EC1R 5BD,
tel. 020 7278 8456, www.viaduct.co.uk

Designed and set by seagulls.net
Printed in Great Britain by Clays Ltd, St Ives plc

A CIP catalogue record for this book is available from the British Library

ISBN: 978-0-718-14953-6

For my husband Jerry,

the most dedicated and focussed worker I know

contents

introduction

If you ever feel overwhelmed by your job, join the club. At some time or other it is easy to be discouraged by the amount or type of work you do, the messy office, the difficult colleagues and the feeling you are getting nowhere fast. In fact, you spend about 1,800 hours a year, almost a third of your waking life, at work and, for many of you, even more. If at the end of the day you don't feel a sense of accomplishment, you can lose your confidence, spend needless time worrying and even become physically ill.

It doesn't have to be like that. In just a few hours, you can make a great start on clearing the clutter which significantly impacts on your ability to concentrate and get things done. Give it a day and you can develop an organized filing system, clean up your computer and arrange your office to use the space you have as efficiently and comfortably as possible. Having succeeded at the easy stuff, you will be up for the challenge of improving your work habits.

One of the greatest lessons I have learned is to break things down into manageable chunks that can be dealt with in short periods of time. It is easy to be overwhelmed with a huge project. Writing a book, for instance. Where do you begin? The thought of 50,000 words is frightening, but ten chapters of 5,000 words each is a lot easier to contemplate. This method holds true for any task you need to accomplish.

To simplify things, I have broken down everything you need to do to clear your space into bite-size tasks with the estimated time it should take you to complete them. Plan a task a day or blitz the whole office in one go, but however you do it, don't stop until you complete it! Finishing projects is the number-one way to bolster your self-confidence and feel a sense of achievement.

Once you get things in order, it is much easier to see where you stand. Breaking old bad habits doesn't happen overnight, but by sticking with a plan for at least thirty days, you begin to get into a routine. I have some fun ideas that really work for keeping you on the straight and narrow, enhancing your time management and other office skills.

You probably like doing some things in your job more than others and find you put off doing the things you don't like to do. Don't we all have moments when licking stamps seems more enticing than getting down to the business at hand? I can be the queen of procrastination and I know how soul destroying it can be to be weighted down with unfinished business. I have also learned that things are never as bad as you think they're going to be, and getting them done is bliss.

In an office environment, aside from the technical skills you need to get on in your job, you also need to get on with your co-workers.

Often job dissatisfaction is personality based. As in most families – and a group of people working together towards a common goal is much like a family – when you spend a lot of time together, you are bound to see each other at best and worst. No one is perfect. Improving your personal communication skills and learning to set some boundaries can help you get on better with your colleagues and make your working day more pleasant.

If, like me, you work from home, there are many other issues you may have to deal with. Not everyone understands that because you are home, it doesn't mean you are available to do other things. People phoning or dropping in can be distracting and may prevent you from accomplishing your goals. In addition to the external distractions, you have a house or flat and maybe even garden, pets or children to distract you. If you can develop a work pattern you can stick to most of the time, you can enjoy the benefits of being able to be more flexible about taking time off. I will share my know-how, along with some tips from some successful home workers I interviewed.

Statistics show that at some time in your working life you will change jobs. Taking the decision to try something new can be very stressful. If you have worked at one place for a long time, you can feel guilty about letting people down. Perhaps you have been made redundant, or moved locations and may be forced to look for new employment. Whatever your reasons for changing jobs, a methodical game plan can help you make a great move. I believe that any change in your usual pattern of life presents a tremendous opportunity for growth. It is a way to revive the excitement that comes with something new and which may have been lacking in your previous position. Trying new things stretches your mind and opens up endless possibilities.

There is obviously more to life than work, work, work. Being able to tune out the work-related issues of the day when you leave your office could actually make you more efficient at your job. It helps give you the benefit of perspective. It is important to use the time you do have off to its best advantage. It's the quality of the time you have and not the quantity that matters. Your social life requires as much planning as your working life and if you maintain this principle, no matter how much time you have off, you will find your life more in balance.

Everyone can gain the benefit from other people's experiences. When I began this book, I interviewed a wide range of people in different parts of the world, in many different professions and at different stages in their careers. I wanted to know how they felt about their workspace, their productivity, their tips for success and the pitfalls of their jobs. There are many routines that successful people have in common that are worthy of passing on, as well as pitfalls to try to avoid, and I have included these in the book with thanks to all.

Finally, writing this book has been an interesting experience as, in the process of asking you to examine your work habits, I obviously needed to re-examine my own. I procrastinated over writing the chapter on procrastination, proving that Americans can understand irony and I had to follow my own advice about letting go of the guilt at not being able to do it all. I didn't always do the grocery shopping or tend to the garden and the world didn't come to an end. In many cases you just have to turn a blind eye and stay focussed on the important.

All the techniques I have described here I use daily. With over thirty years of work experience as employee, boss and self-employed home worker, I have gained an understanding of the skills and disciplines it takes to be happy and successful in a job. I sincerely believe that if you stick to the plan, your work life will improve dramatically in just thirty days.

When you detox your body, you get rid of the impurities that affect your physical health and appearance. *The Great Office Detox* will help you shed the unwanted clutter, attitudes and work habits that accumulate over time and enable you to feel happier and more productive at work.

The rest is up to you. You must make the commitment to improve your own life – you can't rely on anyone else to do it for you. Get started now to feel immediate results. When you take action, you set the wheels of change in motion and the momentum is with you. Experience it for yourself, starting right now.

Dawna Walter

detox your workspace

There is no easier way to feel dramatically better about working or living in any space than to clear it out and clean the area from top to bottom. There is something enormously cathartic about throwing things away that are out of date, organizing the important stuff and cleaning away the accumulated dust and dirt that lurks in every corner. Once done, you will breathe better, gain new perspective and feel more energetic.

You probably have a million reasons why your office is in its current state, but for the moment, I would like you to forget about how it got to be that way, and give me a few hours of your time to begin to get it sorted. There is boldness in taking action and starting and completing a project and you will feel a great sense of accomplishment when you finish.

This chapter is a practical step-by-step guide on how to clear and organize each area of your office. You must remove everything that is moveable from the area you are going to clear and be ruthless at getting rid of anything that is no longer used or required. Don't let your office become a dumping ground for personal items you never take home. Things that sit around and collect dust create pockets of stale and stagnant energy, making your office a more stressful and lethargic environment in which to work.

Each item you put back should be thoroughly dusted, washed, in good working order and necessary to enable you to function in your job. Mend anything that is broken. Broken items represent a break in your business matters. If they can't be fixed, discard them. Assign everything a home so it can respectfully be put away on a daily basis.

Once you have cleared and cleaned, you can begin to look at the layout of your office and ways to make you feel more comfortable and confident in your space. By following some basic Feng Shui principles, it is possible to improve the flow of energy in a space, even if it is not possible to move things around. I will give you quick strategies to make your office a more harmonious environment.

getting started

Before you begin, make sure you have the right tools for the job. You will require sturdy rubbish sacks, boxes, if you are going to archive materials, packing tape, a marker and a cleaning kit consisting of a bucket, J-cloths, rubber gloves, spray disinfectant, all-purpose cleanser, paper towels and a dustpan and brush. A box of bicarbonate of soda also comes in handy to absorb stale odours. Once you've cleared away the junk, you will be able to see what types of kit such as binders, folders or stacking trays are best for keeping your work organized.

It's a great idea to take before and after photos, so plan to bring a camera in to document your progress. The end result will serve as a great reward for your diligent efforts and the photo will serve as a reminder always to keep your office in perfect working order.

Always set aside uninterrupted time to complete each project. Break big projects into manageable chunks so you are not over-whelmed by having to finish a huge task all in one go. You can waste a lot of time and effort just worrying about where to begin! Start with the area that has the greatest impact on your working day.

Make any necessary arrangements to remove the unwanted things from your office the same day you finish. If you are getting rid of lots of heavy things like books and files, enlist someone in the office to help you cart them away.

Do not get distracted by phone calls or e-mails, and don't stop until you finish. You don't have to do it alone if there is a co-worker you can enlist to help. It is sometimes a good idea to have another pair of hands and another viewpoint. If you work in an open-plan space, let everyone around know your intentions. I guarantee you will start a trend and others will follow once they see the finished results.

Brief: Clear desktop *allow 1 hour*

1 Remove everything that is removable from your desktop.
2 Thoroughly dust and clean desktop with water and appropriate cleaning product.
3 Thoroughly edit all items for anything no longer required. Dispose of appropriately and immediately.
4 Only essential items used daily are to be put back thoroughly cleaned.

Know-how

A U-shaped or L-shaped desk is most efficient. Organize your desktop so all your equipment is on one wing of your desk with the computer closest to the corner. This gives you the maximum amount of working space.

If you are a mostly right-brained 'visual' person (see page 11), you like to have your work laid out all around you, which can make your work surface somewhat chaotic. Store your daily work in see-through perspex drawers that fit comfortably on your desk.

If you are a left-brained 'logical' person (see page 11), you work most efficiently with a clear desk. Store your files and paperwork in vertical shelving units keeping your desk completely clear.

Handle your paperwork only once by immediately placing it in the appropriate file.

do you lean towards the right or the left?

The right and left hemispheres of your brain are associated with different functions. We all use both sides of our brains to accomplish everything we have to do, however most people have a leaning towards being right-brained – more creative – or left-brained – more logical. Understanding your natural tendency will help you choose a career that suits your natural way of processing information and can help you find the easiest and best ways to approach problem-solving and day-to-day work responsibilities.

The right side of the brain is more visual, intuitive, able to understand spatial relationships and generally sees things as a whole. People who favour the right side of their brain are good at imagining the end result, recognizing faces, space design and going with their gut feelings. They tend to be more creative and less good at verbal and written skills.

The left side of the brain is the centre of language and is more logical, analytical and rational. People who favour this side tend to work with facts rather than gut instinct, are good at maths, have a large vocabulary and are good at languages.

An exception to the rule can be left-handed people who use both hemispheres equally. The older you get and the more experiences you have doing skills associated with both sides of your brain, the less one-sided you may become.

To see how you can work more efficiently, find out whether you are more inclined towards working with the right or left side of your brain. Tick the phrases that best describe you in each column.

right side
- ❏ I like things to be spontaneous.
- ❏ I am creative.
- ❏ I am good at doing jigsaw puzzles.
- ❏ I remember faces.
- ❏ I am good at reading diagrams.
- ❏ I work better in creative chaos.

left side
- ❏ I like things to be planned.
- ❏ I am logical and analytical.
- ❏ I am good at doing crosswords.
- ❏ I remember facts and figures.
- ❏ I am good at analysing information.
- ❏ I work better in an organized space.

In all likelihood, you will have a combination of both sets of skills; take a look to see if you have more ticks in one column than the other. Does your job enable you to use the skills you find easiest?

Improved energy

Computer and equipment cables and wires that are tangled and in full view bring chaotic energy into the office. Untangle wires and band them together. If possible, tape them under the desk out of sight.

One lovely personal item should be placed on your desk.

A green plant such as a jade or bamboo kept well tended in the left-hand corner of your desk will bring the energy of life into your workspace.

Maintenance

Spend as much time as it takes at the end of each day to show respect to all your business matters by putting everything away in its proper place and clearing your desk.

Schedule a monthly clean-out around the new moon. Mark the date in your diary.

the symbolism of clearing your space

Space-clearing is a ritual found in most cultures throughout the world. It is performed as a sign of respect before sacred ceremonies, or to mark special occasions, in order to welcome the spirits and encourage a positive flow of energy into the space, in much the same manner you would clean your house as a sign of respect before some-one comes for a visit. The simple act of cleaning and straightening up a room shows courtesy as well as regard for the objects themselves.

Clearing your space also helps promote the flow of good chi or energy, as in the practice of Feng Shui. You clear your space not only of the material things that are no longer needed or desired, but also of the emotional vibrations that may be trapped inside it as well.

I'm sure you have all experienced walking into a room and feeling someone's energy. It might be that someone with a big personality has left his or her mark in the space, or perhaps you can feel someone's anger, sadness or an event that took place. You can probably experience some of your own emotions trapped in your space as well. These vibrations can be felt for a long time and can make the atmosphere heavy. In your office space it can make it difficult to get motivated or come up with new ideas.

I have often been asked to help friends out when they are having difficulty in selling their homes – not like my friend the House Doctor who performs magic with their possessions – by clearing the energy in each of the rooms of their house. I usually find the energy is related to the owner's feelings about leaving the house and letting it go. In my space-clearing ceremony I use a sage stick, traditionally used in Native American ceremonies, to help lift the energy of each room, particularly in each corner where it gets trapped.

It is a ceremony that everyone can do and requires just a few simple materials and a quiet five minutes to clear the space. You will be able to feel the difference instantly. One friend sold her house a few hours after I left – and it had been on the market for over six months!

Space-clearing ceremonies are often linked with certain times of the year. In the West, you perform a spring cleaning usually at the first hint of spring as a way of ushering out the winter doldrums and bringing new fresh life into your living space. It is a time of the year when you are motivated to open up the windows and let the fresh air inside, perform a deep cleaning routine in your house by moving furniture and appliances after the dust and dirt of the winter months and bring out your lighter clothing. It is no coincidence that it occurs at the time of year when nature is bursting with new growth.

energize and purify your office space

Space-clearing ceremonies are broken down into several parts – cleansing, purifying and setting the intention for the space. Although I am sure it sounds very New Age, the honouring of these traditions has been practised for centuries. Marking an occasion with a ceremony, such as celebrating a birthday, makes it memorable and fun and adds a joyous energy.

Cleansing

The cleansing process is about showing respect for your space and the objects in it and always begins by removing every object in the area you are cleansing. Thoroughly clean all shelves, drawers and surfaces, paying particular attention to cleaning out the corners. Each item that goes back should be dusted and washed, if applicable.

Be ruthless in getting rid of the clutter. Office clutter is distracting and time consuming. It collects dust and makes it difficult to breathe properly in your space, especially if you have asthma or other respiratory difficulties. Get rid of absolutely everything you don't need with the aim of achieving clear work surfaces.

Purify and uplift

Once you have de-cluttered, cleansed and put things back into your space, you need to remove all stuck and stale energy from the room and invite in positive chi energy. There are many different rituals used to purify space but they all incorporate one or several of the natural elements of fire, water, earth and air. My favourite is a sage stick made up of bound sage leaves that is then burned in each corner of the room. You could also use a candle, incense, feathers, flowers, a plant, crystals or music to help change the vibrations in the room.

To perform the purification: Here is how I perform the ceremony with a smudge stick. You can substitute something to represent the natural elements in your ceremony.

Light the smudge stick and stand in the centre of the room, facing the entry to your office and relax – feel your feet firmly on the ground and take a few breaths in and out to the count of five.

Imagine there is a golden flow of energy coming through the door of your office; it is there to bring new creative life to your workspace. To encourage the flow of this energy throughout the room, walk around in a clockwise direction stopping at each corner and wave the smudge stick in a circle. Imagine the old stale energy rising up and out of the building.

To uplift the space: Beauty is said to attract positive energy so it is important to have something beautiful that catches the eye at the entrance to your office. Other ways of uplifting your office space are with flowers or plants that are well tended, scented candles that use pure essential oils, a bell or music or a silent prayer. All of them do the trick. For a quick uplift of the energy in your office each morning, take a minute and imagine beautiful, gold light in each corner of the room and in all hidden spaces where stagnant energy collects.

Set the intention

The last part of the ritual is to set your personal intention for the space. For example, I look forward to giving my work my best

---

helpful feng shui tips

To allow the maximum energy to flow through your office, follow this quick guide to feel a dramatic difference in how your space feels. Show respect to your business matters and you will reap the benefits.

- entrance to your office attractive and eye-catching
- floor of your office clean and clutter free – nothing to be stored under desk
- never store anything behind doors or in corners; energy gets trapped in neglected space
- desktop free of excess paperwork
- desk arranged so you can see who is entering your office
- back of chair facing a wall to give you strength
- all work filed away at the end of the day
- green plant (jade or bamboo) in left corner of your desk, tended to regularly
- wires organized, neatly arranged and out of sight
- pictures depicting motion
- thoroughly clean and dust office at the end of each week

---

efforts today and I hope to accomplish all I set out to do with great satisfaction and enjoyment. Once you have cleansed, purified and uplifted your space, you have raised the vibrational level. You should now fill the room with your positive energy, your desires and goals.

Stand in the centre of the room in a relaxed stance. Close your eyes for a minute and imagine your enthusiasm and positive energy filling up the whole room. With your eyes still closed, imagine your energy going everywhere in the room. Once you have projected your energy, take a moment to silently declare your intention for the space. Take a few relaxing breaths when you are finished and slowly open up your eyes.

Brief: Clear the backlog of work   *allow 2 hours*

1 Separate the papers into individual subjects.
2 Delegate the tasks that can easily be completed by someone else. Don't interfere.
3 Prioritize the remaining things into the following folders:
   a requires immediate attention
   b can be done in off-peak hours
   c requires thinking time
   d never going to complete
4 Arrange any additional staffing required to get through the backlog. Once you are finished, you can begin something new.

Know-how

When you feel oppressed by the amount of unfinished business and have mountains of papers on your desk, it's time to take quick and decisive action.

Take a maximum of twenty minutes to sort out all piles of paper that have accumulated on your desk. Go with your gut instinct as to which category in point 3 above they fall into. Don't think too much.

List all the tasks you want to complete in your work notebook. Code them as follows:

1 most important
2 time sensitive
3 easy to complete

Spend the next hour beginning to tackle the most important and time-sensitive tasks. These are often the jobs you put off and may be the most challenging things you face. They may include having to deliver bad news, such as having to take an employee to task over something or rejecting someone's suggestions or resigning from your job and the worry that you won't get it right, or realizing you have left something so long it is going to be embarrassing to sort out. Take action and cross something off your list.

Dedicate the first hour of each day to working through the tasks until you get through the backlog. The more time you are able to spend on it, the sooner you will be able to begin new projects.

Thinking time doesn't have to be in the office. Set aside a few hours each week to keep abreast of reading, or go out and gain some inspiration. Any place with natural elements will help you clarify your thoughts. Off to the beach or the park, then!

Improved energy

Unfinished business weighs heavily on the atmosphere of your office making it difficult to relax, concentrate or get inspired by new ideas. Each time you complete a task, you energize the room with your creation.

Maintenance

To have the greatest chance of success, adhere strictly to a daily routine of addressing all your tasks. The more you are able to do things at the same time each day, the greater chance you have to get into a healthy work routine.

Brief: Paper and file management *allow 3 hours*

1 No piles of papers to be stored on any surface.

2 Existing files to be thoroughly edited and organized.

3 Folders created for every type of document you are likely to keep such as projects, training, personnel, personal, suppliers, invoices, events.

4 One in-tray and one out-tray to be looked at a maximum of twice daily.

5 Papers to be handled only once, dealt with and put away.

Know-how

Set up a time each day during non-productive business hours to deal with your paperwork. Stick to the schedule.

Throw away drafts of finalized documents.

Enter all business-card details in your address book and throw away the cards.

Keep all your notes in one notebook. Do not write things down on small pieces of paper. Gather all the notes you've made and transfer them into your notebook.

Limit your correspondence to one page. Ask people to summarize in a page any reports or documents.

If you save lots of information to be read later, designate a time once a week to read. If you never get to it, get rid of it.

Throw out old issues of magazines when the new one arrives. If you haven't read the old one, maybe it's time to cancel the subscription.

Replace all outdated catalogues with current editions.

Keep all receipts in a small envelope to be dealt with on a monthly or quarterly basis as required.

Improved energy

Remove any paperwork relating to poor performance reviews, unpleasant correspondence with co-workers, papers relating to bad business deals past the legal requirement for keeping them. Well-managed files show respect for your business and aid in bringing positive energy into the workspace.

Maintenance

Once you have organized your files, deal with paperwork daily to enable you to have a fresh start each day.

Brief: Books and reference materials   *allow 1 hour*

1 All books and reference materials to be weeded out and those not used in the last six months disposed of.

2 All CDs and other media filed and kept in cases.

3 Reference materials should be stored so that those most frequently used are in the most accessible place.

4 Be sure to keep things visually pleasing. Colour-coding your files and grouping things by height make them easier on the eye.

5 Update your reference library with current editions.

Know-how

Many things that you once needed books to find out, can now easily be found on the Internet. Keep only those reference materials that inspire you or that are truly functional.

If you have more shelf space than filing space, use lever arch files to keep documents for each task in one place, easily accessible and organized. As you finish the task, you can archive any files you need to maintain for client or legal reasons.

Start your own reference files with interesting articles you may find in magazines or trade journals. By keeping only what is interesting, you can rid yourself of surplus paper.

Whenever a new piece of documentation arrives in your office, make a point of getting rid of something that is no longer required.

Improved energy

Leaving room in your bookcase makes way for new ideas allowing a free flow of energy into your workspace.

Maintenance:

Weed out and dust your reference materials on a quarterly basis. When updates come in, clear the files of redundant materials.

Brief: Organizing computer files   *allow 2 hours*

1 Clear your computer desktop of everything but relevant applications and current folders.

2 In your documents folder, set up a file for each project you are working on as well as people files for your most frequent business contacts. You can also set up personal files broken down into categories such as banking, children's schools, etc.

3 File all documents in relevant folders when they arrive. Delete any duplicates.

4 Delete all drafts or redundant information.

5 Delete all incoming or sent e-mails that have been dealt with or require no further action.

Know-how

If you work on a PC, download Google Desktop Tools. It enables you to type in any word or name and will then search through your hard drive and bring up all the relevant files. If you work on a MAC with a Tiger upgrade, the Spotlight programme provides the same functions.

Use your search tool to delete similar items or find things you are looking for, such as all files relating to one project. If they are no longer active but you may need them in the future, use your shortcut to click on all of them, and save them to CD. Delete the files from your hard drive.

Each time you download something from the Internet, your web browser creates a cache of temporary files. You can see this in action when you start to type in a web address you have visited before and the address automatically comes up. If you accumulate too many files, it takes up space on the hard drive and slows your computer. Each browser has a slightly different method of clearing the cache. Go into your search engine and type 'clearing the cache for Internet Explorer' or whatever browser you use.

E-mails can be a major distraction and time wasting if checked too often. Set aside designated times, twice daily, to read and acknowledge all e-mails received. Stick to the scheduled time and don't be tempted to look more often.

Moving something into the recycle bin does not remove it from your computer. You must click on the icon, then click on empty bin. This will permanently remove it from your hard drive. Do this regularly.

Learn more about your computer and become familiar with shortcuts to do tasks more quickly. Even a one-off computer course can help you speed up your work and get less frustrated.

Benefits
You will improve the speed of your computer and the access to your documents.

Removing finished projects and files from your computer gives you a sense of achievement and lightens the load.

De-cluttering your files removes stagnant energy from your computer and encourages new ideas to flow.

Maintenance
✖ Clear e-mails twice daily.
✖ Review project folders weekly.
✖ Add new folders as required.

✖ Back-up and remove old projects on an ongoing basis.

✖ Clear web browser caches weekly.

the e-mail detox

If you consistently have over 100 e-mails in your Inbox, read on. Just as working from a messy office decreases your ability to concentrate and be at your most efficient, retaining too many e-mails, especially in your Inbox, slows down your server and wastes your time. Purging your files of the rubbish takes less time and is far easier to do than sorting through your paper files. Your mail programme can help you sort things out quickly.

Step 1: Create folders

Before you begin to sort and clean through your files, make sure you have created a file folder for each subject of correspondence. Ideally, your e-mail folders will be identical to the system used in your paper filing cabinet. Use the guide you create for your paper files to help you arrange your e-mail folders. To create a new folder, go into the File menu, click Folder, New and name your folder. Use the same names as in your paper filing cabinet.

Create a new folder named 'Waiting to be read' that you can delete when you have finished. To begin with, highlight and drag all outstanding e-mails to this folder.

Step 2: Permanently delete the rubbish

Many people think that when they delete e-mails they are automatically deleted entirely from your computer. In fact, deleting your unwanted e-mails requires further action. Click on Deleted Items and you will get a list of everything inside. Highlight all the e-mails and hit the Delete button, or in Edit on your toolbar click on Empty Deleted Items folder.

Step 3: Edit/Delete Inbox

It's always easier to organize things when there are less of them, so the next step is to go through each e-mail in your Inbox and delete those you no longer need. If there are specific projects or individual's correspondence you don't need to keep, check out the next step to help you review and delete in batches. Don't forget to permanently delete the rubbish daily.

Step 4: Search or Find tool

To continue your detox and help you further organize your files, use the technology. All mail programmes have a Search or Find icon to enable you to quickly find related information. For example, if you want to find all correspondence from a particular person click on Find on your toolbar, choose where to look – your Inbox, Sent Items and so on – and type in the person's name in the From or Sent box. You can also search according to words in the Subject, or the Message itself. This can help you to:

- ✖ retrace your steps on a particular day
- ✖ look for all items relating to one project
- ✖ help you find things you have sent
- ✖ look at all the items received by individual or company name
- ✖ help remove files from the Inbox into an organized folder, easy to retrieve

Keeping the clutter at bay

To block unwanted mail from your Inbox, each mail program has preferences you can choose. Go to your e-mail help program and type in 'block unwanted e-mails' and follow the instructions. You may work for a company that has preset blocks and preferences for security and spam prevention.

I work on a MAC and in the mail preferences I have a tab for rules. I've only just learnt how this works because all of a sudden I started getting a lot of spam e-mails. In the rules you can highlight names of people, words or phrases, or anything you would like to block from your Inbox. Because I was receiving e-mails about Rolexes and other dodgy items, I blocked Rolex and all the spellings the spammers use to get around the block, I have decreased the amount of spam by half. The newest spam is to send the information as a picture file that the block cannot read.

Other ways of eliminating time-wasting clutter:

✖ Unsubscribe from mailing lists you don't have time to read.
✖ Tell your friends not to include you on their chain letters.
✖ Always use the subject line as reference and ask your co-workers to do the same. It helps to easily identify the subject matter and priority.
✖ Save all relevant attachments to your hard drive and delete from your Inbox or Sent items. One e-mail with attachments can go to and fro many times and take up processing space.

---

processing your e-mail

Unless you are in a very time-sensitive business, it is more time effective to address and respond to e-mails twice a day, as you would go through your post or office memos. We all check e-mails first thing in the morning, however, you can choose a time later in the morning to respond to your e-mails after assessing the best way to handle them. Use the same criteria as you use with paper files.

✖ Info: Read and delete unless relevant to ongoing work.
✖ Reference: Read and file in the appropriate folder. Download attachments and save to hard drive. Delete when no longer relevant.
✖ Delegate: Forward e-mail with explanation at the top. Create a folder for delegated tasks and remove from your Inbox.
✖ Action: Take steps to action anything required and when completed, file in the relevant folder.

If you are in a time-sensitive job, you are probably tied to a computer or handheld device at all times and tend to stay live with them. With a BlackBerry, for example, you have the option to delete e-mails from it and still keep them on your computer. Although responding immediately does give the recipient the impression that you are on the case, remember that it is sometimes more important to think about something before you respond quickly.

Efficient processing tips
✖ Bcc if you do not want all recipients to have access to all addresses.

✖ Be sure not to copy everyone into an e-mail automatically. Think about who needs to receive it.

✖ Delete the original message before responding. The sender knows what it is regarding and it will take up less space on both computers.

✖ Do not use abbreviated letters and words – techno speak. Not everyone is au fait with acronyms and it looks unprofessional.

✖ Take some time to think about your response. It's too easy to send a quick reply and regret it later.

Brief: Harmonize office layout   *allow 2 hours*
Know-how

The ideal desk position is facing the door with your back against a solid wall. This is a position of command and enables you to see everyone who is coming towards you. The wall behind you lends you support and security. If you are unable to move your desk and cannot see the door, place a small mirror on your monitor to enable you to see who is coming.

Avoid placing your desk in front of a window. You will feel as if there is nothing backing you up. If that is the only position for your desk, try placing a screen behind you in front of the window.

You must feel ergonomically safe and secure in your office to have a sense of energy flowing throughout your office. Be sure to have your computer monitor or chair adjusted to the right height, so you are looking slightly down on it. Adjust your chair so your thighs are parallel to the ground. Your wrists should be level with the keyboard. For further details, see page 157.

Good lighting is essential to promote a healthy working environment. If there are too many fluorescent lights, you might want to get some removed or get an anti-glare filter for your screen.

If you don't have a window in your office you must represent nature in it to bring calm and relaxation into your space. You can do this with a plant or a picture. If you use a picture, make it an energetic one showing action.

Keep corners, behind doors and under desks free from clutter. These are places where energy can become stagnant.

A dark-coloured rug placed in the centre of your room will help you to stay focussed and grounded.

Improved energy

If you feel healthy and happy in your work environment, you will be more productive and feel more energetic.

Maintenance

Take five minutes at the end of the day to look at your office space and check that each item is back in its place. It is easy to allow clutter to accumulate without even noticing.

once you've completed your clear-out

Take a good look at what you have accomplished and give yourself a big pat on the back. Look at the amount of stuff you were able to get rid of, paying particular attention to the things that had built up due to procrastination. Reflect upon what areas you found hardest to clear out and pay special attention to keeping those areas organized in future.

Ask yourself the following questions:

✖ What equipment do I need to make my workspace a safe and comfortable place to work?

✖ What items do I need to help me stay organized?

✖ What do I need to learn to make my job more satisfying?

✖ What tasks can I get started on?

boosting your physical and mental energy

Clearing away clutter in your office is the first step in helping you feel physically and mentally more energetic throughout the day. Any way you look at it, energy is power. Whether it is the power to make your electricity work or the power that enables you to physically work and move about, finding new sources of energy and learning to maximize its flow will empower you.

To preserve your energy, you must look after and maintain your body through rest, good nutrition and exercise. Your mental and emotional state will affect your energy so it is important to release negative feelings and emotions and develop a positive mental outlook on life.

I am an energy healer and am quite sensitive to people's energy levels. I can physically feel energy flow through my hands and am a great believer in complementary therapies that work on the energy centres of the body. But you don't have to be an energy healer to improve your energy levels. Take this quick test by ticking the options that apply to you and then adding up your total points to see how energetic you are now and take it again in a week's time after avoiding the energy zappers and practising some energy-boosting techniques. You will be amazed by the outcome.

1 *In general, I get a good night's sleep:*
         never 1   sometimes 2 ✓   usually 3

2 *In the mornings, I am generally:*
         lethargic 1   slow starter 2   energetic 3 ✓

3 *I eat breakfast:*
         never 1   sometimes 2   usually 3 ✓

4 *I maintain my energy throughout the day:*
         never 1   sometimes 2 ✓   usually 3

5 *I eat lunch:*
         never 1   sometimes 2   usually 3 ✓

6 *I drink plenty of water throughout the day:*
         never 1   sometimes 2 ✓   usually 3

7 *I find my office energizing:*
         never 1   sometimes 2 ✓   usually 3

8 *My home is relaxing:*
         never 1   sometimes 2 ✓   usually 3

9 *My workspace is under control:*
         never 1   sometimes 2 ✓   usually 3

10 *There are people in my life who zap my energy:*
         many 1   a few 2 ✓   none 3

10–15 You are not respecting your body and your energy levels show it! For the next week, make a conscious effort to get a good night's sleep and to eat properly. Tackle the clutter in your bedroom and clear your workspace during the next seven days.

16–23 Take a look at the questions that you answered which have a score of one. Improve on looking after your body with better nutrition and relaxation, and de-clutter the areas that are not allowing you to feel energized or relaxed. Write down your energy levels in your notebook for the next week making sure you stick to your plan.

24–30 You have good energy levels and look after your body. Look at any areas in which your energy levels feel low and try some of the Energy Boosters on page 35 for the next week to improve the way you feel.

Energy zappers
Lack of food/water
Your body needs the basics to keep your energy levels high. Dashing out of the house without breakfast and eating on the run are both unpleasant and dangerous to your wellbeing. Not drinking enough water decreases your body's efficiency and can cause lack of concentration, headaches and general sluggishness.

Cluttered space
In a cluttered space there are too many things vying for your attention, thus scattering your energy. Clearing your space helps you

concentrate on one thing at a time without any distractions and allows all your energy to flow towards completing your intention.

Procrastination

Putting things off means you can never relax as there is always something in the background consuming a bit of your mental energy. Re-focus your energy into making a list of all the things you need to do to finish one task and don't stop until you get there. Choose something easily achievable.

Unfinished projects

Give up the ghost on things you have put on hold but will never finish and come clean. If it is work-related, ask for help or find someone who can complete it for you. Unfinished things in your personal life can impact on your professional life. Get help for the ones you want to complete and get rid of the things you know you will never do, such as repair old appliances or take up a hobby that you have neglected for years. Letting go of guilt will improve your mental energy.

Holding on to grudges/failures/negative past experiences

Anything negative depresses your energy levels and keeps you stuck in the past. It makes it difficult to maximize the flow of energy and allow new things into your life. The more time you spend thinking about negative things, the more it zaps your energy. Try the release exercise in letting go of emotional baggage on page 186.

Office politics/gossip

Participating in office politics/gossip uses a lot of energy for no great gain. Keeping track of who is doing what to whom is a waste of time and zaps your energy in the process. Focus on your work, not your co-workers, and you will feel much more energetic at the end of the day.

Bad lighting/working conditions

It's hard to feel energetic if your working conditions make you feel physically uncomfortable. Make sure you have a chair that is at the right height for you to sit comfortably and review the ergonomics section of the book on page 157. If your office lighting doesn't suit you, bring an additional lamp into the office. It can also be a decorative feature in your office, providing good Feng Shui.

Take regular five-minute walks to stretch your body.

Negative friends/relatives

We have all known or know someone who can instantly zap your energy. Like an energy vampire, some people have a draining effect. As the saying goes, you can choose your friends, but not your relatives, so if there are friends in your life who zap your energy, see them less frequently. You don't have to hurt their feelings in the process, just distance yourself from them. When you do see them, try to keep things light and energetic. With relatives it is more difficult. Set a time limit in your mind for the visit or phone call and tune out the negative by talking about positive, energetic things such as:

✖ What you have been doing that day or week.
✖ What fun plans you have in the next week.

✖ What you are looking forward to.

✖ Things you've read about or seen.

After a good dose of positive, energetic discussion, turn the conversation around to what he/she has been up to. If the conversation starts to dwell on the negative, move on to the next topic and ignore what was said. I find it works a treat.

Excessive lifestyle

We all have days when we are trying to recuperate from over-indulgence, which obviously impacts on the way we feel physically and mentally. Too much alcohol, smoking, eating too much or too little, all wreak havoc with your energy.

The occasional overindulgence is fun and provides a great contrast in helping you to see how you never want to feel again. The best way to feel better is to rehydrate and eat. When you drink too much, you deplete your potassium levels. Foods rich in potassium help cure a hangover – try a glass of tomato juice, a bowl of pasta with tomato sauce or a banana for a quick boost.

Energy boosters

Food/water

If you are feeling sluggish, the first thing to try is some food and water. Your body is made up of 65 per cent water and you lose it through normal, daily activities, especially in hot weather. The daily recommended water intake is eight glasses a day. Drink water before each meal and spread the remainder throughout the day.

Foods to improve energy and brainpower

✖ raw or dry-roasted nuts

✖ whole grains

✖ fish rich in omega-3: sardines/salmon/mackerel

✖ free-range meat and dairy products

✖ five portions of fruit and vegetables daily – preferably seasonal and organic

✖ healthy carbs: starchy vegetables – corn/potatoes – whole-grain breads/crackers/cereals

Green space/connecting with nature

One of the quickest ways to get a good dose of energy is to go for a walk or relax in a green space. Take off your shoes and feel the grass; make a conscious effort to feel the earth beneath your feet. Imagine you have a hole in the bottom of your foot you can open to suck up physical energy from the earth. Feel the energy slowly rising up your ankles and to your knees. Don't be surprised if you can feel or see the energy.

Grounding exercise: If you have a tendency to feel light-headed but there is nothing physically wrong with you, try this meditation in the morning for the next week before you go off to work to help you feel more grounded rather than always in your head. It will help you feel more connected to what is going on around you.

Sit in a comfortable chair, feet on the ground with you back against the back of the chair. Close your eyes and breathe in for the count of three and out for the count of three; be certain to relax your shoulders. Do this three to five times, until you begin to feel relaxed.

Focus your energy on your feet. Feel their connection to the ground. Now, imagine that you are a tree. Think about what type of tree you feel like today – an oak, a willow, a pine – any type of tree that comes to mind. Think about how tall you would be and then imagine that your roots are growing out of the bottom of your feet into the ground. Take a few minutes to think about what your root system might look like: how deep it is; how far it spreads. You may be able to visualize it clearly, through a mist, or not see it at all simply feel it. It doesn't matter. After you have spent a few minutes feeling your roots, slowly begin to bring your awareness back to your feet. Jiggle them around a bit and in your own time, open your eyes.

Physical exercise

Physical exercise is a fantastic way to get rid of aggression and negative energy. Twenty minutes three times a week can help you alleviate stress and boost your physical stamina. To help release old worries, grudges or work tensions imagine using your out breaths to blow them out of your system.

Laughter/singing/music

Laughing at something is a great way to chase the blues away and give you a definite boost of energy. Keep an emergency tool kit to hand:

- ✖ Call a funny friend and ask to hear a joke. It immediately changes the energy in the room when you have a good chuckle.
- ✖ Pick out three DVDs to buy that always make you laugh.
- ✖ Take a trip to the zoo. Animals always make you laugh!

Music can change your energy levels. Singing increases your energy as does playing instruments. Music can relax as well as stimulate, so take your pick of music to suit the mood and how you feel.

✖ Create a special playlist on your iPod or other MP3 device just for occasions when you need extra energy. What music makes you want to get up and dance?

✖ Do the same for music that helps you relax. Create a playlist of about fifty songs and turn it on when you need to release nervous energy. You won't even have to move to change the album.

Try new things

There is a natural excitement or energy created when you try new things you have always wanted to do. If new situations make you tense, plan over a period of time to fulfil a long-held desire. Taking action towards something brings tremendous energy and with it a great sense of wellbeing. You might decide you don't like it, but the chance that you might is worth taking. It's another thing you can cross off your list.

Clear away a cluttered area of your life

Taking active steps to become aware of your working or living areas by confronting your junk is a great way to feel instantly relieved and refreshed. Always set aside two hours of uninterrupted time and work only on an area you know you can finish within that time frame. The clearing process will help you release negative energy and the clearing of the space will enable a much better flow of energy throughout your working or living space, letting in creative new ideas.

Good areas to tackle are:

- ✖ behind doors
- ✖ under desks/beds/furniture
- ✖ inside cupboards/wardrobes/drawers
- ✖ entrances
- ✖ lofts/garage/spare rooms/storage lockers/archives

what a difference a day makes!

"Lawyers are not renowned for being the most eco-friendly of people, and during the course of a working day I sometimes generate, print and supposedly file, hundreds and hundreds of pieces of paper. When Dawna first walked in, it was clear that there was no real system in place for coping with that sort of paper load; not a single inch of space was visible under the stacks of documents and printed e-mails strewn across my desk.

The detox entailed clearing away all paper which related to matters on which I was not currently working. File it or bin it. One large bin liner later (headed for recycling, I might add), progress was visible. Files were dealt with similarly – the mantra being: 'If they're not current, they should be moved out of your immediate workspace!' Gradually order and control were restored, and by the end of our time together, Dawna had made such an impact that my office was, quite genuinely, unrecognizable.

Only once you feel in control will it be possible to retain control. Two weeks on from my office detox I am delighted to say that my office and my approach to work are reaping the benefits. It is amazing what a difference a clear, well-organized office environment makes to one's attitude to, and enjoyment of, work. I leave my office at the end of the day with a clear desk; a physical sign that I've done that day what I set out to do … and it's been a long, long time since I could say that!

It was with some trepidation that I agreed to let Dawna help me detox my office (after all, I did know where everything was – sort of). But having gone through the process, I can't recommend it enough. It is so much more pleasant to walk into the room in the morning and confront a clear desk and organized paper, rather than feeling instantly overwhelmed by accumulations of undone tasks and undifferentiated masses of paper. Now that I can focus on one thing at a time, I feel more in control – my thought processes are clearer and more efficient and my stress levels very much reduced.

Thank you, Dawna!

I work in an open-plan office and have lots of filing space. Because of the nature of my job, I get loads of information to read – new government agendas, training course information, trade magazines – and process a lot of paper.

I've recently been promoted to team leader which will require me to set up a new team from scratch. I'd love to get myself 'streamlined' to increase my efficiency. I'm actually quite an organized worker, but my desk does not reflect that. I'm a big fan of minimal living at home but find it difficult to have a similar environment at work.

Dawna's Office Detox has provided me with a fresh start for my new managerial role. The benefit of clearing my desk was immediately apparent and I felt a huge weight had been lifted (to the sum of two large recycling bags of paper!).

During the afternoon we went through everything on my desk and in my filing cabinet. The nature of my job meant it was difficult to work towards the 'paperless office' culture my company is striving for. One of the key tips that I'll stick to is keeping a reading tray which should be cleared at the end of each week. I'll also handle each piece of paper or work only once rather than butterflying between documents.

I'm going to use all Dawna's helpful hints to clear out a large filing cabinet – which will assist the new member of staff taking on my previous role. Lots of my colleagues are asking me to pass on tips, so I'll be keeping Dawna updated with progress photos! I'm really excited about my new job and starting it with a beautifully clear desk will help me focus on the new challenges. "

" I knew Dawna was coming for the detox well in advance and therefore I tried to reorganize my office as I was ashamed to show its disarray to its full extent. Nevertheless, Dawna could see where I was blind. She had some sensible suggestions which I should have really thought of on my own, but it was obvious that she had the experience to pinpoint those actions which would make the difference to me.

- Archive files when no longer needed on a regular basis.
- Get rid of Post-it notes by keeping all information in a notebook.
- Utilize the storage cupboards rather than the floor.
- Clearing your desk daily is not time wasting but time saving.

Before the detox I always felt that my office's mess was justifiable because it saved the time spent tidying it up, and I thought I would spend too much time tidying and not enough time working.

I now spend much less time finding things than I used to. I am in control. I do not have hundreds of Post-it notes and pieces of paper lying around and I can find things when I need them. Keeping my office tidy is ultimately time effective which to me has been the greatest improvement.

The weirdest thing is that I feel relieved after having tidied the office.

smarter work not harder

To manage your time effectively you need to be able to prioritize your work and address it in a systematic way. We all have the same amount of hours in the day, so why is it that some people accomplish so much more than others in the same amount of time?

I believe that successful people know how and where to spend their time. They have learned to work on the tasks that only they can do and delegate the more routine tasks that can easily be accomplished by others. They organize their time so the bulk of it is spent on the most important things. Successful people are also adept at adapting to changing circumstances.

I have come across many people who think it is the amount of hours you spend in the office that makes you a valued employee. When I ran a business and had employees who worked late to get their jobs done I just thought that they were too unorganized and inefficient to get finished during regular working hours! All jobs can occasionally demand extra hours, but unless your job specifically requires you to consistently work overtime, it's nothing to aspire to. I find the best employees have well-rounded and interesting lives outside work.

The next step in your office detox is to follow a five-day plan to work more efficiently. Whenever things become too routine, you tend to do things in the same way each day and stop thinking about other options. Not only is it very boring, but it is also unproductive.

It doesn't take a lot of effort to work more smartly. I believe there are a few simple rules you can use to regulate your day that will not only increase your efficiency but will also boost your self-confidence and motivation. It feels so much better at the end of the day to have something to show for your efforts than to be wondering where the time has gone.

Organization plays a great part in smarter working. You have already cleared and organized your office space so the first step is accomplished.

There are four simple rules I would like you to follow each day for the next week which will help you prioritize and achieve your daily tasks and longer-term objectives. Stick to the plan and I believe you will accomplish more in less time and by the end of the week you will feel you really deserve the weekend break as a reward for all you have achieved.

Each of these rules is discussed in detail with simple to follow directions.

✖ keep detailed records
✖ account for your time
✖ write an effective to-do list each morning
✖ Assess yourself at the end of each day

keep detailed records

Writing things down helps you organize your thoughts and records important details in the course of the day. It also provides a handy reference for looking up old information you may need to refer to.

One of the biggest time wasters is not being able to find a piece of information you wrote down. Most people spend an astonishing amount of time shuffling things around trying to find that elusive piece of paper. By writing all information in one place, you will always know where to find what you need.

The type of notebook you use is a matter of personal preference, but make sure it is a size that conveniently fits in your briefcase or handbag, because you should keep it with you at all times. Using the same type of notebook makes it easier to file them away when they are full, and they also look tidier when they are in your bookshelves. It is acceptable to keep individual notebooks for specific tasks such as a phone log or a time log. Put the dates the book covers on the outside.

It is important to write things down in an organized way so you can best utilize the information.

✖ Always write the date, time and names of anyone involved in the discussion.
✖ Give each entry a subject.
✖ At the end of each entry, highlight action to be taken. When possible, act immediately and always note what action was taken.

For the next week, write down the following information in your notebook each day:

✖ Each morning write down your to-do list, numbering the points with the most important first. Break down each activity into all the actions you need to take to start and complete it.

✖ Write down any questions or points you want to cover prior to each phone conversation/meeting.

✖ Take notes in all meetings/phone conversations. Summarize the points and get clarification if needed.

Keep one diary that incorporates all personal and work-related activities

Combining your personal and professional diary is the smart way never to miss important events. It also helps focus your mind on the amount of time you have allocated for each event, helping to keep you on track and on time.

I find the best diary has time broken into fifteen-minute segments with ample room to make notes. I like to keep a diary using pencil so appointments can easily be rescheduled. You can use your computer or handheld devices if you prefer, however, I believe the act of physically writing something down makes it easier to remember.

When you block out time for something, treat it as if you are in an important meeting and can't be interrupted. Let co-workers know you are unavailable and stick to the planned task for the time you have blocked out.

✖ Block out a specific time each day for each item on your to-do list, giving priority to the most important items to get done.

✖ Block out 50 per cent of your time to work on the most important tasks, dedicating up to 30 per cent of that time on the most important if necessary.

✖ Block out a minimum of fifteen minutes' preparation time before each meeting to make notes and gather information – more if needed.

✖ Block out specific times for lunch and breaks.

✖ Leave 50 per cent of your time unscheduled to be able to adapt to daily demands.

Your diary is a great motivational tool. It's important to plan time and schedule activities that fulfil your family, personal and spiritual goals. These events provide great incentive to work hard so you can fully enjoy your time off.

✖ Block out time for one week-night activity and book/plan the activity.

✖ Block out two hours on Saturday and Sunday as personal time to do whatever takes your fancy.

✖ Plan and block out time for a holiday within the next three months, if possible. Twelve weeks will seem within reach and you will work more enthusiastically knowing that a break is to follow.

✖ Block out time in the next thirty days to do the following:
  a Visit your family.
  b Go to at least one cultural thing you enjoy.
  c Have a meal out or at friends' at least once a fortnight.
  d Do one outdoor activity.

account for your time

Time flies, as the saying goes, and in order to become more aware of how much time you spend doing each task, it really helps to account for your time each day. Many professionals bill their time on an hourly basis and their performance is judged on their billable hours. This means that at the end of each day they need to account for all their time and submit it on a weekly basis. In many companies, especially large ones, phone and computer use requires a project code to be allocated so that the time can be accounted for even down to the minute!

Each day for the next week, I would like you to keep track of your time. Keep your notebook on your desk and note when you begin and end each task. If you do the same task at different times of the day, write down when you do it. Also note the time you took for all breaks, including lunch. Here are some of the things you should include:

✖ administrative/clerical tasks
✖ e-mails
✖ looking for files
✖ meetings outside the office
✖ meetings inside the office
✖ personal matters
✖ planning/thinking
✖ post
✖ recruiting
✖ research
✖ supervising others
✖ talking to co-workers
✖ telephone
✖ unexpected stuff
✖ work-related travel

✖ writing
✖ breaks
✖ lunch
✖ Water-cooler moments/socializing

Calculate the percentage of the day spent on each task as follows:

✖ Write down the number of hours you were in the office then multiply by 60.
✖ Calculate the total amount of time you spent on each task in minutes.
✖ Divide the time spent on each project by the minutes in the office and multiply by 100.

For example, you were in the office for 8 hours and 20 minutes or 500 minutes. You spent 73 minutes working on e-mails: $73/500 \times 100 = 14.6$ per cent of your day.

Day one

Once you have calculated what percentage of the day you spent on each activity, do one more thing: look at the list on page 50 and number the points in order of how important each activity is to your day with one being the most important.

Now ask yourself the following questions:

✖ What percentage of my time did I spend on my top three most important tasks?
✖ How much time was spent on unexpected things?
✖ What things did I avoid doing?
✖ What things took longer than I imagined?

✖ What things can I eliminate from my schedule?

✖ What things can I delegate tomorrow?

✖ What things wasted my time?

✖ Did I eat properly and take enough breaks?

✖ What were my accomplishments?

Days two–five

Gaining from the experience of your time study yesterday, make some changes to your schedule today while continuing to keep track of the time spent on each activity.

✖ Eliminate all time wasters.

✖ Plan 50 per cent of your time for specific tasks.

✖ Do anything you avoided doing yesterday first thing in the morning.

✖ Cut down on the frequency you do routine tasks. Do them twice

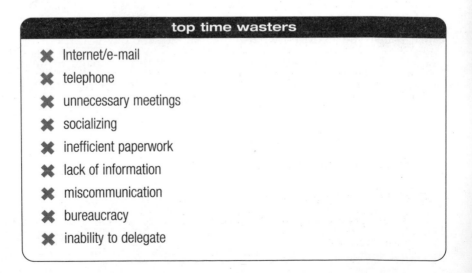

top time wasters

✖ Internet/e-mail

✖ telephone

✖ unnecessary meetings

✖ socializing

✖ inefficient paperwork

✖ lack of information

✖ miscommunication

✖ bureaucracy

✖ inability to delegate

daily at the same time each day when it does not cut into your most productive time.

At the end of the day, calculate your time and percentages and compare these results to the day before.

✖ What percentage of my time did I spend on my top three important tasks?
✖ What things did I accomplish more quickly today than yesterday?
✖ What did I achieve today?

the effective to-do list

To do or not to do, that is the question. You have twenty-four hours in a day and a third of that is spent sleeping, so in sixteen hours you need to be able to balance your work and personal goals.

Your to-do list should start out with a global approach, looking at all the things that you need to do each day. There are many ways to accomplish things on both your work-related and personal lists that will not require too much of your time. Delegating tasks in the office to people wanting to take on more responsibility is a win/win situation. It frees you up to do the things that you can do best and when you do something well, you feel good about it. We will talk more about the art of delegating on page 87.

Follow these simple rules:

✖ Make your to-do list first thing in the morning.
✖ Be as specific as possible about each item so you can measure your success.

✖ Divide the list into two columns – work and personal.

In your work list:

✖ Review yesterday's list and add anything you did not accomplish to today's list.

✖ Write down all the things you want to get done today.

✖ Each day prioritize your lists as follows: A = most important; B = time sensitive but not important; C = if time allows. Your priorities will change on a daily basis, even if you carry things over from the previous day.

✖ Review your list for any tasks that can be done by someone else without your input or supervision. Delegate first thing in the morning and do not interfere.

✖ Always start with the A tasks and, using your diary, block out 50 per cent of your day to work on these tasks only. When you finish your A tasks, continue down your list according to priority.

✖ Break each task down into manageable chunks and prioritize them.

✖ Cross off each item as you complete it.

In your personal list:

✖ Get outside help for household tasks that rob you of personal time. Even a few hours a week relieves some of the pressure and allows you to have a more sociable life. Think about child minders, house cleaners, dog walkers, a laundry service or Internet grocery shopping.

✖ Make it a goal to go to a film or out to dinner, and schedule time accordingly. If you don't actually block out the time and take action, it is easy to become very boring indeed.

✖ Group outside errands by location, scheduling chores in the same neighbourhood at the same time each week.

assess yourself at the end of each day

Devote the last fifteen to thirty minutes each day to review your to-do list and assess your progress. Begin by writing down the number of items on your list. Then count the number you have crossed off. To calculate the percentage, divide the number of items you've written down into the amount of items you have crossed off, then multiply by 100. For example if I had ten items on my list and completed seven of them, I would multiply $\frac{7}{10}$ by $100 = 70$ per cent.

It pays to be realistic about what you can possibly achieve within your given work hours. Setting unrealistic goals or accepting additional work throughout the day that prevents you from achieving your goals is demoralizing and brings your energy levels down, making it doubly difficult to get anything done. The aim of assessing your daily productivity is to learn from your strengths and weaknesses and to do better tomorrow by reviewing the time-management skills you have learnt so far. Write down a concrete plan to achieve it.

If you have achieved less than 65 per cent of the items on your list, ask yourself the following questions:

✖ Were my goals realistic?
✖ Were there any extenuating circumstances that prevented me from achieving my goals today?

✖ Did I follow my written plan to get each task done?

✖ Did I underestimate the time my goals would take to complete?

✖ If not, what prevented me from achieving them today?

✖ What can I put in place tomorrow to achieve the remaining goals?

If you have achieved 65–75 per cent, ask yourself all of the above questions as well as the following:

✖ Did I complete the most important goals on my list?

✖ Did I take on additional work today that I didn't want?

✖ Could I have used more preparation time to complete my tasks?

If you achieved over 75 per cent of your goals, and continue to do that for the remaining week you are on the right path, providing you have set a challenging but achievable workload. We all have the occasional unproductive day, but for the most part, you should be able to achieve 80 per cent of the items on your to-do list most of the time with proper planning and dedication. You must stick to tasks until you complete them so that pattern becomes part of your work ethic. If you consistently do it, it will become routine in a matter of weeks.

review what you have learned

✖ My desk is organized and tidy.

✖ My files are up to date and in good order.

✖ My diary is up to date and has all my activities in it.

✖ My workspace feels comfortable and I have everything I need.

✖ I keep detailed and accurate records of all business activities.

✖ I have eliminated unnecessary work from my routine.

✖ I have cut down on the frequency of performing routine tasks each day.

✖ I have delegated work that can be done equally well by others.

✖ I work on the things that only I can do.

✖ I write down a realistic, measurable to-do list each morning.

✖ I plan 50 per cent of my time daily and write it down in my planner.

✖ I spend 30 per cent of that time on my most important goal.

✖ I prioritize all my goals by their level of importance.

✖ I block out uninterrupted time to do each item on my to-do list.

✖ I start with the most important items first.

✖ I do the most unpleasant tasks first thing in the morning to get them done.

✖ I take time each day for proper breaks.

✖ I schedule in time for my personal interests.

✖ I plan for future activities to keep me motivated.

✖ I account for my time daily.

✖ I look at my successes each day.

✖ I look at better ways to achieve my goals at the end of each day.

out of control days

There will be times when you are so busy you don't know what to do. You have deadlines, your office is a tip, unanswered phone calls and e-mails are piling up – if this sounds familiar, don't panic. The biggest problem is figuring out where to start.

Follow the SOS plan below and at the end of an hour you will feel more in control of your workspace and workflow. It will help you prioritize, calm down and concentrate on, start and complete your tasks.

sos – take control in under an hour
Take a five-minute break

Sit down in your chair, close your eyes and take a deep breath, drawing energy up from your toes, then exhale deeply, blowing out the frustration and worry. Empty your mind of work-related issues, and focus your thoughts and energy on your toes. Wiggle them about and imagine the energy warming them up and then moving up towards your knees. Focus on your knees and continue to imagine the energy flowing up through your whole body bit by bit. When you are finished, take another good deep breath in and out. Slowly open your eyes in your own time. Shake your body around.

The thirty-minute tidy

The state of your office reflects the state of your mind. Clutter vies for your attention and makes it difficult to concentrate on one thing at a time.

Taking action is the best way to get a grip on the situation. In order to prioritize your time, you need to know where you stand. No matter how busy you are, the next thirty minutes should be spent sorting all the paperwork on your desk and immediate area.

✖ Sort all paperwork into relevant categories.

✖ Go through each pile and throw away anything no longer needed.

✖ Create a new folder for each category and label it TO BE SORTED with the name of the task associated with it.

✖ Tidy your work surface and clear your desk.

✖ Look at the files you have created and choose the project that is most important.

✖ Stack all the other files that need attention neatly in one location.

The one-minute rule

Before you begin each task, take one minute to think about what you want to achieve in the time you have allotted it. You can make a list as you go, but do not allow any interruptions during this time.

Ten-minute e-mail catch-up

If you are completely swamped and know you will be unable to address all your e-mails within a reasonable amount of time, it's better to let people know where they stand. Send a short e-mail stating you won't be able to reply fully until a time you feel is realistic and the contact name of a colleague or assistant should anything require immediate attention. If you are going to send it out to multiple recipients, do so as blind carbon copies – Bcc – so each one is received individually.

Attend to any important e-mails and delegate, file, forward and delete as many as you can. An enormous Inbox is clutter as much as an untidy office.

Ten-minute phone catch-up

Listen to any phone messages that may have accumulated and write down in your phone log the details including date, time of call, person, company, subject matter.

Delegate any calls that can be returned by an assistant or colleague. Number the remaining calls in order of priority.

Set aside a block of time – enough to make them all. If you are unable to reach the recipient, leave a concise time when they should return the call. It will save playing telephone tag.

what
motivates you
in your job?

Now that you have sorted out the mechanics of your office, you are no doubt feeling far more enthusiastic, energetic and ready to get things done. This is the energy I would like to teach you to harness for each and every task you have to complete during the day. You're psyched up for the next challenge because it feels really good to see results. Let's look at some ways of keeping the motivation going.

We all work for different reasons, although for most of us money is usually a major part of the equation. Other reasons may be to gain approval, feel independent, contribute to society, express ourselves, learn a new skill or meet new people. Whatever your particular combination is, knowing what you want from your job motivates you to do it.

Most people starting jobs today are likely to change them

upwards of three times during their working life. As new technologies emerge so do new professions to accommodate the fast-paced job market. The choice of career can be overwhelming, especially when you first start out. It is easy to feel pressurized to know exactly what you want to do, especially if you have spent years studying or training for a specific profession.

Take the opportunity to experiment in the early stages of your working life. Try to get as much experience as possible, even if you have to volunteer for a while to get it. If you like the job when working for free, you're bound to love it more when you get paid. When starting out choose the job that is most interesting and gives you the most experience rather than the one that pays the most. The value of the experience will pay off in the long run.

Always follow the path of least resistance, which usually means doing the things you are naturally good at. When your work and your abilities are in sync, you are bound to enjoy the experience more. You are always motivated to do things you are passionate about and it's great to make money at something you really enjoy. This chapter will help you to identify and make the most of your natural gifts in your current work environment and provide the basis for seeking out a job that suits your abilities.

Your personal life will also shape your search for the perfect job. You might want to have flexible hours, work outdoors, or be in a certain geographic location to enhance the quality of your life. If your job and your personal values don't mesh, you'll never feel relaxed and comfortable in your work. We will explore the external factors that influence you in the following pages.

In each job you go through a cycle – initial excitement and fear of not fitting in or failing; adapting to the environment; gaining proficiency; becoming bored; then you begin looking for the excitement again. Don't fret if your job is feeling really routine. There are many ways to make it more exciting and if you have truly outgrown it, you can always move on. We will explore the things you would like to be doing at work and look at ways to incorporate more of them into your daily routine.

It's easy to be motivated to do something you want to do, but it's good to know how to motivate yourself to do something that is not enjoyable. The best way to do that is to plan incentives so you always have something to look forward to. A good example is planning and booking a future holiday – it gives a time limit to complete your work so you can then relax without any worries. Anything you enjoy can be used as an incentive to do your work efficiently on a daily basis.

Don't give up a particular type of job completely if you have one bad experience – try different companies, or work in a different capacity in the same industry. Make sure you fully explore all the options before giving up the ghost and moving on to something new. Each experience helps you define your likes and dislikes and helps you find the one job that is exactly right for you. There is no shame in changing jobs or careers, the only shame lies in not working at something that you feel committed and passionate about, because it takes that kind of commitment not only to be successful but to gain personal satisfaction at the same time.

Get stuck in and have a good look at the things that make you feel good about your abilities, your job and your career possibilities. Then think about the personal things you want in your life in the present and the future. If your current job provides you with most of the things you want, you can find ways to achieve the rest with a bit of planning.

If you find you are not using the abilities and skills that excite you the most, or that your current job no longer fulfils your personal needs, the desire for a change is a great motivating force. When you begin to look for something new you open up your mind to fresh possibilities and see things differently. Whenever you invite different things into your life there is a great surge of positive energy that goes with it.

where do your abilities lie?

The best way to stay motivated is to do things you really like. Because your abilities come naturally, working at something that uses them makes your job easier and more harmonious.

Your abilities are the natural talents or attributes you were born with and which may develop over time. You might be naturally good at something you have yet to discover, so they are sometimes hidden until you try out new things.

It's easy to forget what a talented person you are! Look at the following list of attributes and don't be bashful about acknowledging the ones you possess. Each attribute can manifest itself in different ways; for example, if you are artistic, you might be a great painter or a jewellery maker.

Take a look at the list opposite and tick all the abilities you think you have. Number them in order of importance.

I am naturally:

✖ artistic ✓
✖ athletic ✓
✖ calm
✖ curious ✓
✖ dextrous
✖ diligent ✓
✖ eloquent
✖ entertaining
✖ enthusiastic
✖ intelligent
✖ logical ✓
✖ musical
✖ numerate
✖ organized ✓
✖ patient
✖ stylish
✖ visual ✓

Ask yourself the following questions:

✖ Which of my abilities does my job utilize?
✖ How can I use more of my natural abilities in my current job?
✖ What would utilize my abilities that I would rather be doing?

what skills do you have?

Along with your natural abilities, you have learned many skills through education and practical experience. Although you have a skill, it doesn't mean you necessarily find it interesting. Skills you have learned because you wanted to learn them are more likely to keep your interest when you use them at work. The best learned skills enhance your natural abilities.

Take a look at the list below and tick all the skills you are proficient at. Number them in order of most enjoyable first.

I am skilled at:

- ✖ accountancy
- ✖ administration
- ✖ analysis
- ✖ building/construction
- ✖ caring ✓
- ✖ clerical work
- ✖ computers
- ✖ dealing with the public
- ✖ design
- ✖ direction
- ✖ driving
- ✖ editing
- ✖ legal work
- ✖ marketing
- ✖ merchandizing
- ✖ negotiation
- ✖ photography
- ✖ presentations
- ✖ production
- ✖ purchasing
- ✖ research
- ✖ sales

- ✖ science
- ✖ teaching
- ✖ writing

Ask yourself the following questions:

- ✖ What skills am I currently using?
- ✖ What skills would I like to use more in my job?
- ✖ What other things could I be doing using my skills?
- ✖ What skills would I like to learn?

what do you want from your job?

As your life circumstances change, so do your job requirements. It is always good to be clear in your mind what purpose your job fulfils in your life at a specific moment. Not every job has to be something you want to do for the rest of your life.

Take a look at the list below and tick all the things you want right now from your job. Number them in order of importance.

- ✖ career advancement
- ✖ creativity ✔
- ✖ experience ✔
- ✖ fame
- ✖ financial success ✔
- ✖ flexible hours ✔
- ✖ flexible working conditions ✔
- ✖ fun ✔
- ✖ independence ✔
- ✖ mental stimulation ✔

- ✖ recognition by family/friends
- ✖ recognition by peers
- ✖ responsibility
- ✖ satisfaction ✓
- ✖ social interaction ✓
- ✖ steady salary
- ✖ travel/adventure ✓

Ask yourself the following questions:

- ✖ How am I doing at achieving my goals?
- ✖ What things are missing from my job?
- ✖ How can I incorporate more of what I want into my job?

Look at the top tips at the end of the chapter on page 76 for ways to achieve your personal and professional work-related goals.

what is important to you outside work?

Although some people really do live to work, the majority of us want to strike the perfect balance between our professional and personal lives. Ideally your job will enable you to lead the lifestyle you want while working at something you really enjoy doing well.

Your particular type of job and position within the company will obviously impact on your working hours. If you feel you are sacrificing your personal life for your job, it makes it difficult to give it the commitment it deserves. Fulfilling the non-work-related factors in your life can at times be more important than the job you do, so it is necessary to evaluate where your priorities lie.

Everyone can learn to manage their time more efficiently, which helps get through the workload and frees up some time for a personal life. The next chapter on page 81 looks at time management in greater depth and will help you sharpen up on the tasks that are problematic.

To assess your current work/life balance, take a look at the following list and tick all the non-work things you enjoy. Number them in order of importance. Write down how much time you dedicated to each one over the last thirty days.

✖ cleaning and tidying house ✓
✖ cultural activities ✓
✖ family ✓
✖ fitness/sport ✓
✖ friends ✓
✖ group activities
✖ hobbies
✖ outdoor activities ✓
✖ reading ✓
✖ religious activities
✖ romance
✖ taking classes ✓
✖ time to myself ✓
✖ travelling ✓
✖ volunteer work ✓

Ask yourself the following questions:

✖ Do my job requirements prevent me from doing things that are important to me?

✖ Do I plan time to do the things I want to do?
✖ What do I want to do that I can plan today?

does your job keep you motivated?

After thinking about your abilities, skills and outside interests, you are now in a position to evaluate how your job meets your needs and desires for a happy, motivated work life. Knowing what you want brings focus and clarity and clearly identifiable goals to work towards.

There are many ways to make your job better, even if it does not fulfil all your ambitions at the moment. You can improve upon your skills, become a better communicator and learn to focus on your objectives rather than negative aspects of the job. Your mental attitude plays a huge part in how you feel about your work.

This exercise looks at the things you enjoy and dislike about your job. The things you enjoy motivate you so it is worth taking a look at how much time you spend doing the things you like.

Take a look at the list below and tick all the things you enjoy. Number them in order of importance. Write down how much time you dedicate to each one in an average week.

✖ being part of a team
✖ budgeting
✖ challenges
✖ co-workers
✖ dealing with the public
✖ decision making

✖ environment/quality of workspace
✖ flexibility
✖ marketing
✖ meeting interesting people
✖ negotiation
✖ presentations/public speaking
✖ project work
✖ recognition
✖ research
✖ responsibility
✖ routine
✖ stimulating subject matter
✖ strategy
✖ supervising others
✖ talking on the phone
✖ travel
✖ working on my own
✖ writing

Is there any way to incorporate more of what you like into your week?

Take a look at the list below and tick all the things you dislike. Number them in order of most disliked first. Write down how much time you dedicate to each one in an average week.

✖ being part of a team
✖ budgeting
✖ co-workers
✖ dealing with the public

✖ disappointing people

✖ distractions

✖ environment

✖ lack of recognition

✖ marketing

✖ negotiation

✖ presentations/public speaking

✖ research

✖ routine

✖ strategy

✖ supervising others

✖ travel

✖ working hours

✖ working on my own

Is there someone else you work with who enjoys doing a particular item on your list more than you?

Is there something you can delegate?

Is there a way of changing the task to make it more pleasant?

When you have to do a task you don't like, tackle it first thing in the morning to avoid fretting about it all day.

ten motivational quick fixes

Try these out on any task where you can't seem to work up the motivation to get going!

✖ **Play a mental game.** Tell yourself that you are going to work on the task for five minutes, and in that time give the task 100 per cent. When you finish the five minutes, try another five minutes and you will soon complete the task.

✖ **Tackle any unpleasant tasks first thing in the day.** Think about how great it will feel to have it over and done with and not worrying you for the rest of the day. In most cases, the task is never as bad as you think.

✖ **Turn negatives into positives.** Rather than thinking you don't know where to begin, think where to start and you will find it far easier to get going.

✖ **Give yourself an immediate incentive.** When you really want something, you work harder to get it. Setting a time to achieve your task/reward is an even greater motivation to get it done more quickly. My incentive is taking a break and going out for a coffee, but whatever you look forward to will work for you.

✖ **Compete with yourself.** See how much better you can do something now than you could do it in the past. Self-satisfaction is the best motivator of all.

✖ **Talk about the task with someone you find motivating.** Other people can be a great source of motivation. Chat with a co-worker, expert, friend or family member who may be able to offer advice on how to best achieve your goal.

✖ **Do something you can start and complete quickly in between difficult tasks.** You will be enthusiastic when you have completed it and ready to face something more challenging.

✖ **Take a minute to visualize the end result.** Use your imagination to stimulate you into action. Close your eyes and see yourself finishing the last bit of what you are doing. Be as specific as you can in thinking about what it looks like, how it feels to have finished it and what a great job you did!

✖ **Think about a new project you can begin when you complete this one.** Finishing up old business makes way for new energy, and the desire to do new things can help motivate you to finish old tasks.

✖ **Imagine getting a big pat on the back from your boss or colleagues when your work is done.** Everyone likes being praised for a job well done. Being eager to please a co-worker can give you the added enthusiasm you need to start and finish your work. If your boss or colleagues forget to show appreciation, give yourself a pat on the back for finishing what you start.

top tips to reach your career objectives

Career advancement

✖ Discuss your career goals with your supervisor or the human resources department in your company.

✖ Ask for additional responsibilities.

✖ Take courses that will advance your career. Ask your employer to help with any costs or arrange in-house professional training.

✖ Look at different jobs within your company that will enhance your experience.

✖ Write a current CV and boost your self-confidence by looking at your work achievements and skills.

✖ Research other companies in the same field and see if there are any that would complement your talents and experience.

✖ Be prepared to take a risk. There is something very exhilarating about doing new things. Go with your gut feelings when you are thinking of making a career change.

Financial success

✖ Your lifestyle should reflect your current earnings not your future potential.

✖ Future-oriented people are the most successful. Save a percentage of your monthly salary for your future goals – a house, car, retirement, etc. Investments reap financial rewards.

✖ If you feel you deserve a pay rise, ask for it. In more cases than not, you will get something. Know what you are worth by comparing your job to similar jobs listed on websites or in newspapers.

✖ Always keep in mind your work/life balance and don't trade one for the other.

✖ Make a list of your short- and long-term goals. For each goal write down as many ways as you can think of to achieve it. Try them out starting with the easiest first.

Flexible working conditions

✖ Set the parameters for the working conditions that suit your lifestyle.

✖ Be upfront with your employer about any conditions you may have regarding your work such as hours, travel or any part of the job you can't do. If they can't accommodate you, it's not the job for you.

✖ Companies do not want to lose capable employees, and given twenty-first-century technology, many companies are willing to look at flexible ways to keep you on board. If you want to change some of the parameters of your current job, write down your proposal, think about the benefits to the company and present it to your boss.

Mental stimulation

✖ Utilize all the facilities available to learn as much as you can about your areas of interest.

✖ Ask for more complex tasks or added responsibilities.

✖ Find a mentor with lots of experience who you can bounce your ideas off.

✖ Focus on developing a new idea for at least fifteen minutes a day. Do it at the same time each day.

Recognition by family

✖ Keep your family up to date about what's going on at work. The more they understand what your job entails, the easier it will be for them to be proud of your achievements.

✖ Invite them to your workplace. Plan a lunch or bring them to a special event when they can see you in action – they will surely be impressed.

✖ Be empathetic. Listen to the daily work experiences of your partner or other family member and recognize their work contributions as well.

✖ Not everyone is able to verbalize his or her feelings. If you can't see signs of recognition, it doesn't always mean people aren't interested. Engage them by asking how they think you are doing.

Recognition by peers

✖ Ask your supervisor/manager to evaluate your performance on a regular basis. Ask about your strengths and what areas need improvement, then work on these.

✖ Be enthusiastic. When you bring energy to your workplace, everyone will feel comfortable and energetic in your presence.

✖ Come up with a new idea or improve upon an existing one. Clever and industrious people leave a mark.

✖ Work for the good of the team. Team players fit in and make management's job much easier.

✖ Look at company-wide competitions you can set as your target to win.

✖ Become active in an organization linked to your profession.

Self-satisfaction

✖ Find a job doing something you love and everything else will fall into place.

✖ Start and finish everything on a timely basis.

✖ Give each task your best, no matter what it takes.

✖ Write down your achievements at the end of each day.

✖ Share your achievements with the people who mean most to you.

✖ Celebrate your achievements with frequent rewards, even if they are small ones.

staying on top of your work

Take a deep breath. By now you should be feeling a whole lot more organized than you were before you began – just by clearing the clutter and following a few simple routines to help you work more smartly. Your office should feel peaceful and comfortable to work in. Sticking to this space-clearing routine as best you can for the next thirty days will help you to master it, and besides, you will continue to get good results and feel better at the end of the day.

As great as it would be for life to run smoothly every day, the reality is that things crop up that require or divert your attention and you end up having a very different kind of day from the one you had planned. Learning to manage the outside influences that impact on your time is the key to achieving your existing work goals while coping with day-to-day challenges. You must also learn to accept that some days will be a complete disaster and that tomorrow is another day.

Your diary is the most effective tool for helping you keep on track. By scheduling the exact time you plan to tackle each project on your daily to-do list, you really focus your mind on what you hope to achieve in a specific and measurable way. At the end of the time allotted for the task, you can see how well you did. The more you practise sticking to your time plan, the easier it will become to get your work done within that period of time. It really does work!

The benefit of valuing your time in this manner is that it also gives you a clear picture of the free time you have available to take on new assignments. Rather than squeezing something new into your existing schedule, it's easier to be able to plan to do it at a time when you have completed existing tasks and can give it your full attention. When you feel in control of your workload, your job becomes more rewarding and a lot more fun.

Sticking to your game plan takes a lot of discipline, as well as the realization that you can't control everything and do each thing well. If you are reluctant to give up some of your less important tasks because you don't feel anyone can do them as well as you can, think again. Learning to delegate the less important tasks gives a co-worker an opportunity to gain further experience and allows you to focus on what you do best. If you try to do it all, you will always fall behind and feel utterly overwhelmed.

Throughout this chapter we will look at some of the ways you can easily lose control of your time due to *external* factors and some tips to help you acquire the skills needed to finish your planned tasks as well as dealing with the unexpected. The following chapter will deal with procrastination – the *internal* ways you avoid doing the tasks on your schedule.

why take on new work?

One of the easiest ways to stray off course is to take on additional responsibilities. You might do this for many reasons: to impress others; because you don't know how to say no; because new projects add mental stimulation and challenge to the job. The downside can be that you put the less interesting projects on the back burner and fail to complete the projects you identified as the most important. In some cases you may not have a choice and will be required by a boss to take on a new assignment. For whatever reasons you add work to your schedule, it helps to do it intelligently. Take a few minutes to get to grips with whatever the assignment entails. You will then be able to break the task down into manageable chunks and fit it more easily into your existing schedule.

Before accepting new work, ask the following questions of the person who requires the work to be done:

✖ What is the deadline?
✖ What exactly is entailed?
✖ How long should it take to do?
✖ Do I have all the information I need?
✖ May I check my schedule and see if the time frame is realistic?

After reviewing the answers, ask yourself the following questions:

✖ Am I putting off doing something more important to take this on?
✖ Can I achieve the time frame required?
✖ Do I need additional help to accomplish the task?
✖ Am I sacrificing my personal life to do it?
✖ Why do I want to do it?

By taking the time to analyse the requirements of any new task, you can formulate an honest opinion as to whether you are able to complete your own work as well as the new assignment. If something's got to be sacrificed in the process, it is better to be upfront at the start. Once you can assign a project a beginning and end date, it makes it easier to work it into your schedule.

Investigate some of the reasons you may take on additional work. Put a tick next to any of the reasons that you have taken on additional responsibilities. Number them in order of importance.

✖ prove to myself that I can do it
✖ impress my supervisors
✖ impress family
✖ learn something new
✖ mentally stimulating
✖ help out a co-worker
✖ more pay
✖ can do it better than anyone else
✖ don't want to upset the boss
✖ don't know how to say no

If any of these reasons have caused you to bite off more than you can chew, the added responsibilities were not worth it in the end; you can disappoint yourself, co-workers and family with the best intentions in the world.

The following techniques will help you stick to your plans and manage the unexpected to best suit your time and skills.

how to say no nicely

In an effort to please everyone, you often say yes rather than being honest and just saying no. It is understandable you don't like to disappoint people but, in saying yes, you often don't have the inclination, time or energy to do what you've promised. It's a lose/lose situation that you should try to avoid. It is possible to learn to let go of the guilt of refusal and stick to your plans.

The greatest tool you have to be able to say no with conviction is your written daily diary. By writing down a specific time to do the important things in your professional and personal life you have the perfect reason to decline new work or personal commitments that conflict with your schedule. The more you are able to stick to your plans and set your boundaries, the greater chance you have of staying on track with your career and personal goals.

When you are asked by a supervisor to take on something urgent, be clear and upfront about your current time commitments. Discuss the following with them to set the record straight:

✖ Point out the important tasks you are working on and the deadlines associated with them.

✖ Ask for help in setting your priorities and how the task fits into your current projects. Discuss the implications of achieving other deadlines in light of the new workload.

✖ If you don't think you can deliver your usual high standards given the time frame, be upfront so as not to disappoint.

✖ Suggest someone else you feel may be able to handle the task or help share the burden. Suggest you delegate and manage rather than do the hands-on.

✖ Look at your schedule and see what time you can reasonably give to the effort and not neglect your prior agenda. Be specific and say 'I can give you two hours between x and y' and allocate that time to that one task.

✖ Present an alternative by telling the person when the best time to do it would be – such as tomorrow or next week. You can then plan the appropriate time to get the job done well.

✖ If you pitch in and work extra hours, take that time off at a later date to do something special. It will make the effort worthwhile.

✖ People will remember you letting them down far longer than they will remember you saying no upfront. Honesty is always the best policy.

When you have to say no, do it nicely. It's always better to deal with people in person or on the telephone rather than saying no by e-mail or a text message. I believe that when you say no you should offer some explanation as to why you can't do it this time. Explain the demands of your schedule and ask that in the future, when possible, they try to give you more notice so you can plan it into your schedule. Offer alternative times or dates that would suit you.

When you have to say yes to something you'd rather not do, the only way to get through it is to tackle it straight away. The more you think about how much you don't want to do it, the more difficult it will be to begin. Spend a few minutes getting your head around what is expected of you and write up a quick outline – manageable chunks of the project – with an estimate of how long each item will take. Group like things and do them all together.

what and how to delegate

I have always believed the more you allow others to learn about what you do and help you do it, the easier it becomes for you to take on more responsible jobs that allow you to excel. I'm sure there are some tasks that only you can do, and for the most part, these are the things you should be concentrating on. There are some tasks, however, that may not utilize your skills to their best advantage. Everyone wants to move up the career ladder by learning new skills so, by delegating some of your workload, everyone wins.

Delegating works not only in your business life but also in your personal life. When your time is at a premium, you will feel much better if you can use it for doing things you really enjoy rather than tasks that take up time and aren't rewarding. You can get help to do household chores, look after the kids, walk the dog, do the laundry and even help you with a fitness routine. One of the great motivating factors for working hard is to be able to afford the pleasures that are important to maintain your balance. Delegation is an art. You need to take time upfront to teach the skills required to do the job and you need to clearly verbalize what is expected. The more specific you can be, the greater chance there is of getting what you want. A good example would be – one-page report due on the fifteenth of the month. By specifically stating the length and time frame expected, you give a clear goal that is achievable.

Here are a few rules to follow when delegating work:

✖ Delegate the end result, not the methodology. Everyone works differently to achieve the same result so allow your assistant to do the job as they please.

✖ Explain the importance of the task. Everyone likes to feel they contribute to the group effort.

✖ Once delegated, do not interfere. Be clear that you are available if needed, but allow the person to get on with it.

✖ You can show interest by occasionally asking how it's going.

✖ Delegate tasks that are not the best use of your time. These may include some things you enjoy doing but are not productive, such as checking and responding to routine e-mails, telephone calls and correspondence, all of which can divert you from your core work.

✖ Don't delegate for the sake of delegation. Things that can be eliminated from a routine are just time wasters.

✖ Always delegate the right task to the right person. The ultimate goal is a successful result.

✖ Allow assistants to do some important tasks such as the preliminary analysis on a report or problem. Getting another perspective and input can help you formulate more informed results.

✖ Remember that it is a learning process for your assistant. Point out ways in which the result was good as well as ways of making it better. You were a novice once!

✖ Always acknowledge other people's contributions to your overall effort. Sharing the glory will make everyone feel a part of the team and will go a long way towards gaining future cooperation.

If you have a hard time delegating, let's look at some of the reasons you may find it difficult to let go:

✖ You don't trust anyone to do it as well as you.

✖ You worry that someone may do it better than you.

✖ You think it will take more time to show someone else how to do it than do it yourself.

✖ You don't think anyone would want to do it.

✖ You are embarrassed to ask for help.

These are areas that you need to work on, because holding on will keep you standing still rather than moving forward. In order to have new energy and new projects, you need to have a flow of work out and in. To help you delegate in the future, identify co-workers who would like to advance their careers and dedicate a few hours each week to teaching them the necessary skills to eventually take over some of your responsibilities. They may not get it right at first, but the investment of time will be worth it in the long run.

doing other people's work

Being an assistant is one of the toughest jobs in the office, one of the least recognized and most important. Assisting work colleagues or members of the public requires an unflappable nature and pleasant easy-going personality.

Although the management in most companies take the big decisions, without assistants sorting out the details even the greatest corporate leaders of the world would not be able to accomplish what they do. In fact, unless you are the very top dog of your company, you will all be required to assist those above you in some aspect of their job. Whether your permanent role is to assist another member of staff or you are called upon to assist your boss in some activity, only good organizational skills will enable you to juggle the many projects you have to take on board.

Entry level assistants will probably not have a great deal of experience dealing with a busy office, but whatever their skills, they impressed someone enough to be hired. They will be a bit nervous about getting things right at the start, but if they are interested in the work and want to move ahead in their career, they will be eager to please.

If you have an assistant to help with your work, treat him/her with respect. If you have many assistants, take the time to know each one and where they are on their career path. It is incumbent upon you to teach and mentor in return for them taking some of the more tedious and time-consuming tasks off your plate.

Take into account the level of experience each assistant has. If you feel that one can take on added responsibilities, groom them for a job promotion that will inspire them further. Be clear about the things they need to master to achieve a step up and be sure to assess and direct them clearly and concisely.

Assistants are not slaves, thank goodness, and shouldn't be expected to wait on you hand and foot. Unless your assistant controls your diary, screens your calls, and is more of a personal assistant who enjoys running your life, don't expect them to take on personal non-work-related chores. Reverse roles often and offer to get the tea, pick up a sandwich or post the post. Seeing things from both perspectives helps you gain greater understanding. Always take the time to say please and thank you and acknowledge their contribution to your efforts. Be certain to give praise – it makes for a happy and contented team.

If you are a full-time assistant, it is very important when you begin your job that you have a good understanding of what will be required. If a job description exists, make sure you read it properly and put it away in your file.

Ask questions and develop an open-door policy with your immediate boss that enables you to get answers to things you don't understand. Be realistic about the time frame it will take to complete a task. It's better to be honest than to disappoint. Learn how to say no, nicely. If you work for more than one person, start and complete one assignment before beginning the next. Try to keep it on a first come, first served basis rather than allowing people to pull rank. Of course, if something is urgent, you will have to follow the instructions of your supervisor.

Be interested in whatever you are assigned. Become a sponge for information and learn all the ins and outs of the business. Keep your eyes peeled for learning opportunities and educational programmes offered through your employment and think about what you would like your next position to be.

Although your job description will list some of your expected responsibilities, be prepared for the panic and occasional crises that befall work environments when all hands are on deck and most rules go out of the window.

A great assistant will exhibit most of these characteristics:

✖ great organizational skills
✖ ability to prioritize work
✖ understanding of deadlines
✖ good social skills
✖ enthusiasm
✖ eagerness to learn
✖ understanding of the way their boss works best

✖ loyalty

✖ discretion

Things to desire in a good boss:

✖ clear-cut instructions for all tasks

✖ realistic deadlines brought about by good planning

✖ please and thank you

✖ acknowledgement of your contribution

✖ patience

✖ respect

✖ helping you towards advancement, if desired

tips for time management

The more structure you develop in your daily routines, the less time it will take to think about how to approach things. Putting in place a specific format to use in writing reports, preparing for meetings, dealing with your correspondence and phone calls will help you formulate your thoughts easily, keep them organized and retrieve information quickly when you need it.

The one-page summary rule

The most effective way to accomplish this is almost like playing a game of word association. Think about the requirements of the project and take five minutes to write down everything that comes to mind without censoring or judging your responses. Once you have put down everything you can think of, you have the basis for an outline. You can now number the points in order of relevance –

and refine the list by crossing off items that are not important to the end result. Use this technique when you have to write a letter, a CV or report.

This one-page summary now becomes the basis for any further work that may be required and is a document you can pass on to your supervisor or members of a team to show how you propose to address the project. It keeps everyone informed and keeps the project defined and on track. It is also advisable to institute this as a policy for how you would like to receive information. It is always best to be straightforward with co-workers and in the long run it will produce far more effective communication within your organization. Ask for a one-page summary of any meetings, reports, financial data and you will save an enormous amount of time each day.

The more precise you can be in limiting the scope of your work, the easier it is to focus your mind on providing the right information. For example, to prepare a one-page summary rather than a twenty-page report helps you focus on the most important aspects of the information. The end result is a clear picture rather than something with bells and whistles that masks the important information. It saves time in the preparation and makes it a lot easier for the recipient to digest.

The effective meeting

Unnecessary meetings can be a huge source of irritation within an organization and can waste countless hours a week. A clear-cut agenda and good timing can alleviate meeting overload and boredom, saving time and resources to work on more important things.

Challenge the necessity of a face-to-face meeting if the task could be handled more efficiently without one. If the meeting is outside the office, you have to add journey time which eats into your day. If you can arrange a conference call, for example, you can get the job done without wasting time.

If you are required to participate in a meeting, ask the following questions well in advance:

✖ What is expected from my participation

✖ What information do I need to bring?

✖ When will I receive an agenda?

✖ Can I offer my points prior to the meeting?

✖ Who else will be in attendance?

✖ How long is it likely to run?

Discuss any concerns prior to the meeting with the person in charge rather than other participants. This is a good way to keep politics outside the meeting room and work towards a successful conclusion to the agenda.

When you are in charge of the meeting:

✖ Send a notice of the meeting in good time so everyone can attend and prepare.

✖ Ask colleagues for any items they wish to include on the agenda.

✖ Prepare a one-page agenda to be distributed in advance.

✖ Stick to the agenda to enable you to measure the success of the meeting.

✖ Begin the meeting by stating the points you are going to cover and explain when you would like to answer any questions. This will keep interruptions down to a minimum.

✖ Start and end on a positive note.

✖ To restrict the meeting time, schedule it towards the end of the day when people are anxious to get home.

Setting responsible response times

You are bombarded with information and requests for your time every day in both your professional and personal life. Never before has it been so easy to get in touch at a second's notice anywhere in the world. You can be reached by landline, mobile phone and e-mail not only from your computer, but your BlackBerry and handheld mobile devices. You can use specially fitted phones on many long-haul flights and there are very few places, if any, where you can't be contacted. Is this good, I ask?

I must confess my personal prejudice on this topic up front as I live with a BlackBerry addict. I have observed the phenomenon over the last eighteen months and have witnessed what I can only describe as people who must not have any personal life. E-mails are sent and responded to within a minute at all hours of the day and night. I can't help but wonder whether it is a teacher's pet syndrome – showing your unending commitment to the job. How good can the information that is being passed on possibly be, without a second's thought given to the matter?

Although it is important to respond to all communications you receive in a timely manner, preparing a response should require some thinking time. Writing down the points you want to cover can help you prepare succinct and correct information to be passed on at an appropriate time. As long as it is received when the information is needed, try to stick within working hours. Always take a minute and put yourself in the receiver's shoes. Will they get it in the middle of dinner or the middle of the night?

Only you can judge how important each communication is likely to be. You can delegate all written or telephone communication an assistant can deal with and focus on those only you can respond to. It is better to have an assistant return a call to say you won't be available to speak until a scheduled time than not to return the phone call until you have time. Everyone likes to have closure and know where he or she stands. Some tasks may be less pleasant than others and those should be done first thing in the morning as a matter of priority.

* ✖ written correspondence: one business day
* ✖ telephone calls: within forty-eight hours
* ✖ e-mail/BlackBerry: not before fifteen minutes have elapsed
* ✖ e-mail/computer: within twenty-four hours
* ✖ in-house request for meeting: one business day
* ✖ external request for meeting: within two weeks

the dreaded syndrome: procrastination

The obvious way to conquer procrastination is to tackle the things you hate doing first thing each day and get them out of the way. You will release all the anxiety that may have built up about them and can then get to grips with the remainder of your day without worry. It's easy to say, but sometimes more difficult to put into practice.

Why do we procrastinate? The simple explanation is that we put off doing important things for emotional reasons usually based in fear – of disappointing, not being perfect, being too successful and having to live up to expectations, or the fear that you don't know what you are doing and someone will find out. Sometimes it's because we don't like someone telling us what to do, or we simply don't like doing particular things. The downside is that whatever you haven't done will hang over your head and, until you take action, it will make you feel bad.

Basically there are two types of procrastinators – those who worry and get tense about putting things off and those who are laid back and put the task out of their mind altogether to do something more pleasurable. The laid-back procrastinator doesn't feel guilty.

If you are a worrier, you can feel overwhelmed by pressure. Your fear of failing makes it difficult to begin tasks and you put off doing them because you worry about where to begin. You have a difficult time acknowledging your accomplishments and are afraid to take risks and can be very indecisive. You may also be a perfectionist.

If you are more laid back about the effects of your procrastination, you have learned to con yourself into believing that nothing is really so important that it can't wait. Because you are so good at tricking yourself, you don't really see the need to change unless you are confronted by a crisis and must deal with the reality of the situation. Laid-back procrastinators can only break the habit when they are good and ready to.

Here are the most common ways to procrastinate. Take a look at the list below and identify which ways you most use in procrastinating.

✖ You substitute a less important task for the one you know needs doing.

✖ You use excuses to put it off: 'I'll have more time tomorrow.'

✖ You put it out of your mind completely and opt for something that is fun.

People who become tense and worried about certain types of tasks regularly use the first two ways to procrastinate. Different types of fears associated with tense procrastinators are covered below with easy ways to help you be more proactive in combating your procrastination.

People who tend towards the third method of procrastination can be very selfish and don't see the effect of their lack of action on others. They seek instant gratification, want to be part of a crowd and have a tendency towards laziness. Although it is difficult to get a laid-back procrastinator to focus on important things, it's not impossible. In addition to the time-planning skills learned in previous chapters, there are ways to get laid-back procrastinators to re-evaluate their priorities further in the chapter on page 117.

fear of failure

Let's face it, no one likes to fail at something, yet no one is perfect and all of us will fail at some things and succeed at others. The problem with worrying about failing is that it can stop you dead in your tracks before you even begin. You end up missing out on some great life experiences just because a particular thing might have gone wrong in the past and you are too afraid to try again. Staying within your comfort zone is also a fear of failure because you never test yourself to see if you can do better and always feel disappointed in your achievements for never having tried for more.

The fear of failure can also manifest itself physically and you can become ill when you are about to undertake something that frightens you. Common symptoms include: headaches, nausea, digestive problems, elevated blood pressure and asthma. Basic relaxation techniques can be helpful in alleviating the physical symptoms, but once you conquer the fear and tackle the task, the physical symptoms will subside.

Some failures will be more significant than others. If you have invested a lot of time and energy into something that ultimately proves unsuccessful, it can shatter your ego and cause you to question your path or direction in life. Yet every highly successful entrepreneur has had his or her ideas shot down at some stage of their career. The key to overcoming a fear of failing is to learn from the experience and move on. Don't take things to heart, but use your brain to gain knowledge and do better next time around.

It's difficult to believe that failing can be good for you, but the reality is that if everything was perfect all the time, life would be boring. You need contrast in your life to help you develop your preferences and refine your dreams and ambitions. When you fail at something, the first lesson is to try harder. The second lesson is that you can't be great at everything and there are some things you might have to acknowledge you will never be able to do. It's better to face reality than con yourself and always be disappointed.

People often set themselves up for failure by taking on more than they can possibly achieve and therefore never feel any sense of accomplishment at the end of the day. The fact they have so much work becomes a rationalization for not being able to succeed and they get into the endless cycle of expecting to fail and subsequently do! The work we have done in the past chapters on setting realistic goals and standards should help you focus on getting the important tasks done to a good standard and on time.

Never take delight in another's failure. On some level, this emotion makes you feel less bad about your own failures, but can also be used as an excuse not to try to reach your potential. The media seem to delight in reporting the rise and fall of successful and famous people. The higher up the ladder they are, the further they have to fall. It takes a thick skin and a lot of confidence to stand up and put yourself on the line when you see others torn to shreds. The rewards, however, are great.

Ways to combat fear

It's not as bad as you think: You often build up an unrealistic picture of the task you are putting off doing, imagining the worst possible outcome. In reality, it's never as bad as you think it is going to be and the relief when it's done is sublime. The more you think about it rather than doing it, the longer you prolong your misery. An easy way to begin to conquer your fear about a task is to create a picture in your mind: take a minute to think about the advantages of getting the task completed and the reward you can give yourself once it's done! Big tasks deserve big celebrations.

Now, take a few minutes to sit quietly and take a deep breath in and out to the count of five. Keep your shoulders relaxed and your feet on the floor. Imagine you know exactly the best way to accomplish your mission. See yourself easily writing down the key points you want to achieve. See yourself completing the writing, phone call, presentation or anything that you need to do. You feel confident and relaxed and the task is taking a fraction of the time you imagined. When you are feeling happy, begin to bring your awareness back to the moment. Wiggle your toes, shake your hands and slowly open your eyes.

Take the next five solid minutes of effort to break down your task into manageable chunks. Spend another five minutes on it then put it down for an hour. Then give it five more minutes' full effort, then another five. Try to extend the time by five minutes each time you tackle a bit of the task.

To give yourself a quick boost, do the same mental exercise but this time recreate a successful event that has already happened. Think about it in as much detail as you can and go through the whole process from start to completion in your mind's eye. When you are re-experiencing the joy of finishing something you are proud of, begin to bring your awareness to the moment. Wiggle your toes, shake your hands and slowly open your eyes.

What's the worst that can happen? Fear of failure procrastinators can often conquer their fears by being prepared for the worst. In fact, many professionals, such as lawyers, doctors, bankers, analysts are trained to look at all possible options, the worst-case scenarios included. Armed with the ability to deal with all potential outcomes, the procrastinator can feel more comfortable about taking action. This method is more time consuming and causes a bit of stress in living out negative outcomes that may never happen, but it can help develop a methodical approach to taking risks and trying new things.

Listed below are some common fears about undertaking a task you keep avoiding. I'm sure you can add a few more things you worry about. To help feel prepared, for each point write down five ways you could fix the problem if it did occur.

✖ I'll get it wrong.
✖ I won't meet the deadline.
✖ I'll need to ask for help.

> ### quick tip
>
> You will, in the course of your professional and personal life, make mistakes, get angry, hurt and disappoint those you love and those you work with. It just happens. The best way to come to terms with it is to take full responsibility for your actions. 'I'm sorry' goes a long way to helping you through tense situations and can make even the most disappointing news easier to deliver or accept.

✖ I'll disappoint someone.
✖ I'll make someone angry.
✖ Everyone will think I'm stupid.
✖ I'll get fired.
✖ People will laugh at me.
✖ I won't get an opportunity to do it ever again.

An example of ways to fix the problem would be:

✖ If I get it wrong, I'll ask where I went wrong and get clear advice on what is required.
✖ I'll calculate how much time it will take me to fix.
✖ I'll ask for the help I need to get it done successfully.
✖ I'll block out enough time to sort out the problems as a matter of priority.
✖ I'll stick to the task until I complete it on the day it was promised.

Confide in a buddy: When you fear failure, typically, you keep it to yourself. Your demeanour does not have to be shy and retiring to fear failure. Outgoing and confident-looking people can be self-doubters deep inside. If you have more bravado you are more likely to give it a go, even with the self-doubt, although you can still go through the worry or physical symptoms leading up to taking action.

Keeping your fears secret enables you to replay an irrational fear over and over again in your mind without the benefit of perspective. By learning to verbalize your fears, it helps de-bunk the fear and work on ways to overcome the problem. When you gain perspective from someone whose opinion you trust, it can help you put your mind at ease. This is a very straightforward approach to begin over-coming your fear of getting things wrong.

A strategy that really works is the buddy system. You tell your best friend about something you are afraid to tackle and promise to listen if they have a problem. You then ask your friend to schedule gentle reminders that can help spur you on. It can be a phone call during the day or even a text message to let you know that help is at hand. Just being able to express your doubts or gain new input will give you more confidence to stick to the task.

Think about the tasks you worry about doing and for each one, write down a person who you can talk to about it. Ideally, you should choose someone who has experience in dealing with the task and can also share with you the benefit of his or her own experience. Everyone is flattered at being deemed an expert, so asking for help compliments them and helps you out in the process.

Take your failed experience to your head, not your heart: Our fragile egos want to be loved by everyone and we believe that by getting things right all the time we will be loved and appreciated.

When things don't go according to plan and you fail at a task, you may think of yourself as a failure. Associating love and acceptance with constant success will put you under undue stress and make you an emotional wreck. In my experience, women are more likely than men to take things to heart and wear their emotions on their sleeves when things don't go according to plan.

The best way to learn from failure is to approach it analytically rather than emotionally. Use a bit of creative role playing to help you overcome your feelings of personal rejection and look at the situation more realistically.

Pretend you are a researcher doing a report on whatever it was you failed at. As a researcher, you are there to get the facts and draw conclusions based on them. Ask yourself the following questions:

✖ Was there a written remit for the project?
✖ Was the remit followed?
✖ What areas of the project were done well?
✖ Was the project started on time?
✖ How much total time was spent on the project?
✖ Was the project adequately researched?
✖ What could have been done to make the project better?
✖ Were there more skills required in order to do this project?
✖ Was there adequate communication with co-workers?
✖ Were there personality-based issues?

Look at your answers and prepare a new action plan to tackle the task again with the benefit of knowledge gained from the experience. Give the second time around your best effort and if it leads to a successful outcome you have benefited from the failure. If you fail again, there's no shame in that. If you still have the desire to do it the third time around, be sure it is something you really can and want to do. If you meet all the physical and mental requirements for doing the task, keep trying until you succeed. If you have to accept you are not able to do it, concentrate on your core strengths and move on.

Keep track of the things you put off doing because of worry: Most times worry about failing is based on irrational concerns. A good way to get over this fear is to keep a diary of your thoughts and feelings about the tasks you procrastinate over. For each task, keep the following details:

✖ Write down the time and date of each journal entry.
✖ What worries me about this task?
✖ What excuses have I used to avoid doing the task?
✖ How long have I avoided doing it?
✖ What will happen if I do the task?

Look at ways to address the concerns and use the 'what's the worst that can happen?' exercise to work through the concerns you have. By reviewing your journal – say weekly – you can identify your patterns of procrastination and alleviate the distractions you have allowed to divert your attention from the important tasks you put off.

paralysed by perfection

There's nothing wrong with striving to get things right, but being a perfectionist means you measure your worth solely on your achievements. If you get things wrong you are absolutely devastated. You set unrealistic goals and measure your success by unrealistic standards and constantly feel disappointed in your accomplishments.

Perfectionists are the worst procrastinators. The fear of not being perfect and not living up to your own expectations as well as the expectations you feel others have of you, makes it really difficult to start a project or try anything new.

Perfectionists are very uncertain of their own abilities and are indecisive. If you are a perfectionist you always seek the perfect solution to a task or problem and ask for several outside opinions before being able to take a decision. It takes you a long time to do your work and, as a result, you put things off and then beat yourself up for putting them off, and the cycle continues.

In reality, there is no perfect way to do anything. Each individual adds the benefit of his/her experience in tackling a task. No two people will do something in exactly the same manner and there is no one correct way to do most things. The easiest way to learn is by making mistakes and taking these on board until you have learned thoroughly. Invention comes from trial and error, and it's both the trying and the errors that push the boundaries to help create new things.

Ways to combat paralysis by perfection

Get used to losing: A gentle way to get you to worry less about winning (being the best) and losing (anything other than being the best) is to engage in a game with some friends a few hours a week and view it as a sort of therapy. Anything will do – backgammon, charades, trivia, bowling, even karaoke – anything that is light-hearted and meant to be a laugh rather than a serious competition. The best idea is to play with friends who are on the same level! The more you play, the more you will be able to see that the laugh (or the journey) is more important than the end result. There will always be someone who can play better, faster or have the luck of the draw. You will soon discover that the world does not come to an end as a result of not being the best.

Laugh at your mistakes: Saying things out loud enables you to externalize and release some of the pressure. Looking at the funny side of any situation and sharing it with someone you trust will help lessen the stress associated with it. Things that seem catastrophic in the moment, given the benefit of time and perspective, prove to be nothing at all.

People in the public eye often make fools of themselves and survive to tell the story. There are numerous television programmes that focus on mistakes and blunders from people in politics, the media and the general public. From my personal experience in broadcasting I can tell you that mistakes happen all the time, and can be really funny, even though they may be painful when they happen.

To gain a bit of perspective and find the humour in your not so perfect moments, take a few minutes to think about three mistakes you have made in the past that upon reflection are quite funny now.

Ask yourself the following questions:

✖ Were there any long-term effects on my life by having made the mistake?
✖ How did I feel about it at the time?
✖ How do I feel about it now?
✖ What did I learn from the experience?

Don't punish yourself for failing: If you are a perfectionist, you are your own worst critic. You believe that unless something is perfect, it has little or no value. To begin to overcome these feelings, it helps to acknowledge the achievements you make on a daily basis, even if they are small ones.

At the end of each day, try to view each task realistically and write down all the steps you took to achieve them. Only look at the positive steps and not time you feel was wasted.

Share your accomplishments with a person you trust and care about. It's not bragging to tell someone what you achieved in the day. View it as preventative medicine that will help you to focus on the positive rather than the negative.

fear of success

Suffering from a fear of success can begin early in life if someone is born with special gifts and talents. At an age when there is great comfort in fitting in, it can be very disturbing to be singled out for your achievements. This can lead to a form of procrastination where you deliberately avoid doing things you are good at so you can be normal.

Being part of a successful family can also give rise to the fear of being successful. You feel you must live up to the family reputation as well as developing your own. This type of intense pressure can make it very difficult to follow in the footsteps of your elders or peers. You can observe the sacrifices successful people often make when it comes to having to choose between business or family obligations. If you grew up in this type of environment, you may be determined to shy away from seeking success because it represents long hours and absence from home and family.

Sometimes fear of success can be gender based, especially when you work in a role traditionally held by the opposite sex. Women can feel that if they are too successful they may scare men off whereas men working in roles typically held by women can feel their masculinity threatened by too much success in a women's job.

Successful people can also be insecure. Having achieved success, you can feel as though you don't deserve it and feel guilty for being recognized for your achievements. If you have reached the pinnacle in your career, you can get to a point where you feel you can never achieve anything else because you have already done everything and can procrastinate about trying new things. The pressure of people's expectations coupled with the internal pressure you place on yourself to succeed can be overwhelming.

Ways to combat fear of success

Define your short-term goals and objectives: If you worry about future success, the thought of all the effort it requires over the long term can be daunting. As with all tasks, breaking the big, insurmountable problem into smaller units you can cope with, enables you to go at your own pace to achieve the happiness and fulfilment you desire.

Looking at your life as a whole, make a list of all the things that would make you comfortable and happy right this minute both in your professional and personal life. Focus on the small things that don't require a massive effort to achieve but still require good planning and sticking to a schedule. The more you are able to realize your short-term goals without the worry of having to give up something in the process, the easier it will be for you to begin looking at the long-term picture of what you ultimately want to achieve in your life.

Find a successful role model: Not all success brings pain and misery. To be able to do something you are passionate about well is the level of success we should all aim for. You don't have to have buckets of money, live in a big house or be famous to achieve success.

To overcome whatever fears you may have about being too successful, take some time to look for positive role models who have a successful career without making the sacrifices that worry you. Think about friends, family or someone in your profession you admire and set up a time to chat. Discussing your fears is the best way to get over them.

rebellious/nitpicking procrastinators

Rebellious procrastinators put off doing things by constantly questioning why they need doing in the first place. They feel hard done by and singled out for unpleasant tasks and, in general, spend a lot of time being angry and not liking their job. They are constant complainers and can be difficult to have as co-workers.

If you get angry and defiant about being asked to do things, you have some issues with control. These can date back to when you were a child and can be something you have struggled with for a long time. We all go through rebellious stages where we struggle for independence. However, if you always believe you are right and find it impossible to accept anyone else telling you what to do, best go off and work on your own.

Ways to combat it

Think about others before yourself: Your strong self-belief makes your focus inward without taking notice of the effect you have on others. When you constantly disrupt the flow of work just to make your voice heard, you take up everyone's time which could be better spent on getting the job done. When you leave things until too late, you tend to create a crisis or nitpick about insignificant aspects of the work so as to shift the blame to others.

Take a look at whether you constantly fight battles that don't exist and spin your wheels rather than moving forward. Confronting reality and taking responsibility for your own actions by looking at other viewpoints and recognizing everyone's contribution to making things happen can soften the rebellious edge.

Ask yourself the following questions:

✖ Who is affected when I procrastinate at work? List everyone by name.
✖ Who has to make up for the work I don't do? List everyone by name.
✖ Do I keep regular working hours? If not, how often are you late?
✖ Do I stick to deadlines? List the percentage of times you miss deadlines.
✖ Do I know more than other people who do the same job as me? If yes, list the names of people you are smarter than.
✖ Am I smarter than my supervisor? If you answer yes, list the ways.
✖ Am I given work that is beneath me? If so, list.

✖ Has the same thing happened in previous jobs? Think about your previous jobs and see if your attitude towards that job was the same.

I hope at this point you will see the negative impact that your rebelliousness has on those around you and that you can take full responsibility for your actions. Acknowledging your mistakes would be a great way to say sorry and put it behind you.

If you sincerely feel you have more skills than other people, you're in the wrong job and it is time to put your money where

---

top tips to avoid procrastination

✖ Start with a tidy desk.

✖ Remove all known distractions from sight.

✖ Do things little and often. Give the task five minutes of devoted time to make a dent. Repeat every hour, trying to increase the time by five minutes.

✖ Look forward to starting rather than worrying about finishing. The anxiety comes with the deadline. By getting excited to begin, you get your creative mind in action to help you with the solutions.

✖ Make an unpleasant task fun. Plan an immediate incentive when you finish.

✖ Set time limits for making decisions. The more time you have, the more time will be spent worrying whether you will get it right.

✖ Schedule time to play so you don't feel deprived. A relaxed mind can think better and get tasks done more quickly.

✖ Repeat this mantra – I don't have to be the best.

your mouth is. Go to chapter 9 on page 189 because it is time to make a move.

Relieve the mental tension with physical activity: The best way to work out anger and frustration is to replace a negative activity with a more positive action. Physical exercise helps relieve the physical symptoms of tension and clears the mind as well.

If you find that things are heating up, take a brisk twenty-minute walk. Rather than stew on the problem and make it worse, observe everything that is going on around you. Imagine you can take great photographs by blinking your eyes and capture the moment. When you get back to your office, sit down for a few minutes and write down what you saw.

You can also try some breathing exercises to help when you are feeling angry and tense. Go back to the grounding exercise on page 36 and sit quietly for a few minutes before you begin.

what do you procrastinate about?

Take the procrastinator's challenge to identify what things you procrastinate about. Tick each thing on the list you avoid doing until you absolutely have to, and when you are finished, number them beginning with the thing you procrastinate about most often.

✖ taking decisions
✖ confrontations
✖ carrying out major plans
✖ changing or taking risks
✖ delivering bad news

✖ dealing with paperwork

✖ returning telephone calls

✖ sticking to a time schedule

✖ saying what's on your mind

✖ trying new things

✖ moving on in career/personal life

✖ filing/admin

Now they are out in the open. Take the list and put it somewhere you can see it – the dreaded Post-it note on the computer – and don't allow yourself the excuses you make to avoid tasks. Look at the underlying emotions you associate with the task and the ways you can work at combating fears and eliminating pressures.

DO IT NOW!

encourage others not to procrastinate

It is impossible to change another person's habits, although it doesn't stop most of us from trying! The only thing that changes habits is the desire of the individual to make that change. Until he/she becomes aware of the behaviour and takes active steps to change it, the behaviour will continue.

Procrastination never feels good physically or mentally. It creates stress and lowers self-confidence and is one of the leading energy zappers in the workplace. Helping your colleagues to get on top of their work can be very rewarding, but don't feel a failure if old habits die hard.

Here are some helpful hints to urge them on.

Lead by example

The best way to encourage change is to set a good example. Your efficient work habits can encourage others to work in a more efficient manner. When you are always punctual and respect your co-workers' time and efforts, your colleagues are more likely to follow suit.

If you have a particularly good methodology for getting your work done on time, share it with your colleagues. You might think about planning a lunchtime seminar on how to organize and prioritize your workflow. Ask your company if they will provide the lunch – everyone likes a freebie!

When relying on colleagues to contribute to your work, be very clear about what is required and when it is due. Be as specific as possible in the methodology you expect and provide a time line when each aspect of the project is due. Break the big task down into manageable, smaller pieces so that the procrastinator knows where to begin.

Security deadlines

To guarantee the work will be done on time, request it is completed well in advance of when it is really due. Although this is a somewhat deceptive tactic, it will give you some spare time should your colleague not comply with the deadline date.

When a colleague misses a deadline, it is fair to discuss with him/her how his/her work habits impact on the rest of the team. Ask the following questions:

✖ What prevented you from getting the work done on time?
✖ What help do you need to organize your time better?

✖ What skills do you need to better understand your work?

✖ How do you think your procrastination affects others?

Progress reports

Although the purpose of farming out projects to co-workers is to give you more time to do the things only you can do, keeping on top of the outsourced work will lessen the likelihood of disappointment.

Depending upon how far off the deadline may be, require a synopsis of a few paragraphs on the status of the project on a daily or weekly basis, depending upon the size of the project. When a colleague knows that he/she needs to progress daily rather than putting it off until the very last minute, you are more likely to get timely results.

Praise

Because people who procrastinate are often lacking in self-confidence, building up your colleague's self-esteem through praise is a sure-fire way to encourage the desired results. Go out of your way to praise even the smallest bit of progress. Try to do this on a daily basis. When people feel you have their best interests at heart, they feel less threatened and are more likely to perform well. Be sure to share your colleague's progress with other people on the team and even with your boss. The more people who acknowledge their efforts, the more confidence they will gain.

Provide incentives

Everyone works better when there is something to look forward to. The more motivated your co-worker is to complete the project on time, the greater the likelihood they will succeed. The more successes under their belt, the easier it will be to gain compliance in the future.

Incentives should be given for completing work *ahead* of the due date and the incentive should be something relevant enough to matter to the colleague. Here are some suggestions:

✖ nice lunch/dinner out of the office
✖ leave work early for a day
✖ come in late for a day
✖ tickets to an event
✖ help with career advancement

office
dynamics

Your work colleagues are like your daytime family. Some of them know how to wind you up, some you fear, others are supportive and some you probably compete with. Like your family, they get to see you at your best and your worst and, because you all spend so much time together, you can see their strengths and weaknesses as well. People working in close proximity will often have periods of tension as egos and objectives collide.

There are, however, great differences between family and colleagues. Within a family structure you have deep, emotional bonds and your reactions are based on emotions first and facts later. Ingrained childhood habits often surface when dealing with your family but would not be appropriate in the workplace. In the work environment, no matter how close you become to your co-workers, your reactions should be based on fact first, and emotions should be kept out of the scenario altogether. I'm not saying it is not good to be passionate or have strong views on things; it's just not good to react to situations based on emotion.

A fun part of your job should be that you get to interact with people who share the same interests as you. Working with people is a great opportunity to learn new things and gain experience from observing how more experienced people tackle their assignments. Socializing with work mates and developing team spirit can enhance the work experience so much it can be so much fun you can't believe you get paid to do it!

There will always be personalities that never mesh with yours. Managing difficult relationships can be tricky if you carry the baggage from past unpleasant encounters into each new task. A good office detox can flush out the old systems for dealing with difficult people and help you focus on the objective and not the personality.

This chapter will help you define your role within your organization, rid yourself of work habits that offend your neighbours and help you become a terrific team player.

the role of the boss

There are all kinds of bosses and the reality is that they are not all perfect. A great boss should inspire you and help you reach your maximum potential because he/she knows that by letting you contribute as much as possible to the company, he/she will also shine in the process. There is a whole range of other types of bosses.

No boss possesses the ideal combination of skills to handle every single aspect of their job. Backing up the boss, depending on the size of the company, are the key people in the organization and the teams that back them up. The person at the top is ultimately responsible for overall performance. How senior you are in your company and how big the team is, will dictate where you stand in the pecking order. In theory, each individual does the relevant tasks to make the entire operation work smoothly and efficiently.

There are some basic skills that every boss should possess, especially if the company is small and everyone relies on each other to make the business run smoothly. Personalities being what they are, it doesn't always go according to plan. Whatever skills you feel are lacking in your boss, the odds are, you will never change his or her habits and you can waste a lot of time, effort and emotion trying to. The smart route is to learn to change your reactions to your boss's behaviour to enable you to deal more effectively with the situation, or alternatively, move on.

I have worked in lots of different environments, in public and private sectors, both as an employee and a boss. In the course of forty years' work experience, I have been through my share of office and boardroom politics, scary bosses, difficult co-workers and tense environments. I have also been lucky enough to have some great bosses and colleagues who were generous with their knowledge, time and encouragement. The good ones stick in my mind whereas I have forgotten about the terrors.

A good boss, to my mind, has most of the following skills:

Good verbal communicator
✖ makes sure you know your role within the company
✖ picks the right time and right place to communicate
✖ looks you in the eye
✖ listens as well as speaks

✖ checks you understand what is said in a non-threatening manner

✖ comes to chat occasionally to see how you are doing

Gives directions

✖ clarifies the task and the deadline

✖ points out potential problems

✖ discusses specific ways he/she wants the project done

Takes decisions

✖ fair and reasonable in decision taking

✖ gives adequate thought to each matter

Delegates and lets go

✖ doesn't interfere

✖ checks progress when appropriate

✖ available for help

Accessible and approachable

✖ you feel comfortable around your boss

✖ you feel he/she will make time to meet you

✖ you can share your career goals

✖ you can share any problems

Organized

✖ gives you ample time to complete work

✖ keeps accurate records

✖ sends out written information on a timely basis

✖ knows what's going on in the office

Open to suggestions
✖ actively encourages everyone's ideas
✖ implements other people's ideas
✖ asks for your opinion

Encourages learning
✖ understands that learners make mistakes
✖ offers learning opportunities within the company
✖ offers outside learning opportunities

Gives credit where credit is due
✖ encourages achievements
✖ gives team credit to his/her superiors

Able to help with your weaknesses
✖ interested in your growth and helps you reach your potential
✖ supportive when pointing out areas needing improvement

Upbeat, energetic motivator
✖ promotes team spirit
✖ plans incentives and rewards
✖ gives individual praise and recognition

Harmonizer
✖ puts the right personalities together
✖ treats each employee fairly
✖ doesn't show favouritism
✖ doesn't promote negative competitiveness

Accepts blame when due

✖ takes full responsibility for errors

✖ admits mistakes

If you are the chief honcho, give yourself an honest assessment of how well you do at each of the skills listed above by rating yourself on a scale of 1–5 for each one, 5 being the highest score.

If you want to know how your staff rate you, why not do an anonymous questionnaire using these criteria to see what they really think of your abilities? Compare how you see yourself to the way others perceive you and you can improve on the areas that may require some work.

rate your boss questionnaire

Rate your boss on the above skills. If you don't feel your boss has a particular skill, give a zero rating. Try to keep personality out of it and keep strictly to the skills listed above. Add up the points and see how your boss rates. At the end of the scoring are some suggestions of how to deal with challenging bosses.

0–19 If your boss really scores this low, it's time to find a new job. Waiting for him/her to change could take a mighty long time and you are probably so unhappy you are not gaining much from the experience.

What you have learned is the types of skills you rate as important in a boss. The interview process in a job search goes two ways – not only do prospective employers get to see whether you will fit into their company, you get to see how you feel about them. Gut instincts are a good basis to begin with.

20–35 There are some crucial elements missing from your work experience. In each area you feel your boss is lacking, you need to employ strategies to obtain the information and help you need to get your job done well and give you a sense of accomplishment at the end of the day. Utilize the strategies listed on page 130 to compensate for your boss's weak areas and see how you get on. When you reach the point where you don't feel you have anything new to learn from this work experience, get your feelers out for a new position – maybe even in the same company. Chapter 9 on page 189 will help you get your skates on and not settle for mediocrity.

36–49 This score paints a picture of your average boss – better at some things than others, but someone who is generally in control of what is going on and mostly pleasant to be around. To make the most from this type of environment, you need to be self-motivated and stick to your goals, because you may not always be presented with opportunities or receive the recognition you feel you deserve.

50–65 Aren't you the lucky one! Your boss is a gem and the ideal role model to learn from. Share your long-term career goals with this person and you will be well on your way towards achieving them.

how to make the most of a difficult boss

Bad verbal skills

✖ Reverse roles and clarify the points as you understand them.

✖ Put things in writing before and after meetings. Always start with: 'I understood from the meeting/phone conversation that ...'

✖ Don't interrupt. After your boss finishes, try to sum up the conversation as you understand it.

✖ Try not to take to heart any verbal dressing down made in the presence of co-workers. Some bosses are notorious for not dealing with matters privately. If your boss does it to you, he/she probably does it to everyone, so let it pass.

Lack of direction

✖ Don't wait to be told, ask. You can take a few minutes to think about how you would approach a particular task, write it down, then ask if this is right. If not, ask how they would like it done.

✖ Seek advice from a colleague on the same level as you or higher.

✖ Be proactive. Look at the work schedule for the next week/ month and anticipate what may need clarification. Put your questions in writing and set up a time when you can discuss the answers with your boss.

Unapproachable

✖ Look for co-workers who get on with the boss and find out what works for them.

✖ Your boss is probably not as bad as you think. We all have bad days. Take a few deep breaths, think about a positive outcome, put a smile on your face and learn to approach your boss when you need to. The more you communicate with him or her, the easier it will be for you.

Unorganized

✖ You have been practising your organizational skills throughout the book, so be the leader. Know your deadlines, ask for work in advance and keep good written records you can distribute when appropriate.

Dictator

✖ If there is only one way of doing things in your work environment, you either suit it or you don't. Some people are perfectly happy being told exactly what to do, whereas others need to have more creative input into the work routine. You will never change a dictator-type boss so you have to live with it or get out.

Credit monger

✖ If your boss is a credit hog, there is probably nothing you can do to change it. It is very important you recognize your own achievements and set rewards to make them memorable. Keep an on-going record so you can add them to your CV.

Bully

✖ If your boss is prone to make fun of employees' failings, promotes an unhealthy atmosphere of competition in the office and always shifts the blame, the only course of action other than leaving is to discuss your concerns first with your boss, and then with the human resources department of your company. Life is too short to be miserable, so you either have to find ways around it, or chalk it up to experience and move on.

the role of the employee

Whether you are employed on a part-time basis or work at a senior level in a big company, there are certain codes of practice that all employees should honour; in every job you do, you should strive to do your best, no matter how insignificant the task may seem.

Your role, no matter what your job, is to represent the company you work for. As such, you need to dress and act the part. As a representative of your company, you speak on their behalf – so whatever you say about the company should be in its best interests. It is better to say nothing than to say something negative.

When you are at work, keep things professional. Although we all get the occasional personal phone call or e-mail throughout the day, work must take priority. I often experience receptionists taking personal phone calls while ignoring customers who are waiting. If they worked for me, they wouldn't be doing it for long!

The following characteristics and skills make up the things I would look for in a good employee. They are listed in the order I think are most important.

Honesty and integrity
Honesty and integrity are two things every individual has complete

control over and, to be a good employee, must practise on a daily basis. Whatever you say or do not only impacts on your personal reputation, but also on the reputation of your company.

- ✖ keep confidential information confidential
- ✖ don't promise what you can't deliver
- ✖ admit when you don't know something
- ✖ keep your word and always follow up when you say you will
- ✖ don't speak behind someone's back
- ✖ voice your concerns about anything to the appropriate person

Enjoys the job

The best employees really enjoy their job and take pride in their work. They also add fun to the workplace, and a jolly staff is always a more productive one. A good giggle every now and then goes a long way in making a happy place to work. A good employee:

- ✖ looks forward to getting to work
- ✖ gets right to the task at hand
- ✖ is eager to learn new things
- ✖ helps out in order to learn
- ✖ never complains
- ✖ is proud member of the company

Good time-keeping skills

When you make an effort to be on time, you show respect for the job and those around you. Most companies rely on the skills of their employees to keep things running efficiently. When you have an unscheduled time delay, other people often have to pick up the slack.

We all have occasions when unavoidable circumstances mean we are late for a meeting or with a deadline. Those circumstances can be mitigated by communication with the affected parties as soon as you are aware of a problem. However, when you are constantly late or unrealistic about your time, you need to review the previous chapters on working more smartly and planning your day. A good time keeper:

✖ arrives at work on time each day
✖ takes only the allotted time for lunch/breaks
✖ meets deadlines
✖ is on time for meetings
✖ keeps to personal schedule
✖ returns phone calls/correspondence in timely fashion

Pleasant personality

Something as simple as smiling really can go a long way in raising the energy levels of your work environment. Like yawning, smiles are contagious and can even be felt from a distance – over the phone and in correspondence – and, by being pleasant, you can even soften a difficult blow.

Pleasant people are more fun to be around. They are generally in a good mood, optimistic, helpful and observant. A pleasant colleague:

✖ says good morning/goodbye to co-workers
✖ knows everyone's name and job
✖ shows respect for authority
✖ always says please and thank you
✖ optimistic/looks on the bright side

✖ helps out wherever needed
✖ points out co-workers' achievements

Good appearance

I have read several surveys that show how much appearance influences promotions and pay, no matter how much an employer may deny this is the case. In studies done both in the UK and America, results show that handsome and taller people rose through the ranks more quickly and earned more money throughout their lifetime.

You don't have to be endowed with great physical looks to have a great appearance. By looking and feeling confident, you can gain the same benefits in the employer's mind as someone with dashing good looks. If you pay attention to your personal details, you will give an appearance of being a details-oriented employee who reflects well on a company. They show this by having:

✖ hair clean and groomed
✖ face clean and groomed
✖ hands and nails clean and tidy
✖ well-fitted clothing respectful of your position
✖ clothing and shoes clean, pressed and polished
✖ no excess make-up/aftershave/scent

Knows how to prioritize

✖ works independently on important things first
✖ deals with the urgent
✖ delegates to appropriate staff
✖ follows up on the routine
✖ re-assesses at the end of the day

Good communicator

✖ expresses thoughts clearly verbally

✖ expresses thoughts clearly in writing

✖ listens, giving undivided attention

✖ asks for help when needed

Helpful/takes initiative

A sure-fire way to make your mark in a company is to be a doer. By that I mean the kind of person who pitches in to help out – even if it's not part of the job description or even if it means getting a cup of coffee – nothing is too menial for the helpful colleague.

When you take initiative, you are using your creativity to seek out new areas of opportunity. All great employers like creative thinkers because they add new energy to the company, helping it to grow and expand into new areas. They:

✖ look for things to do when finished own workload

✖ spend some time each day creatively thinking about new opportunities

✖ volunteer for tough assignments

✖ learn new skills to advance career

✖ ask for constructive feedback

rate your skills as an employee

Do you give your job your best efforts or are you just collecting your salary? If you aren't enjoying what you are doing, you should be doing something else and now is the time to take action.

For each of the traits or skills of a good employee listed above, rate yourself on a scale of 1–5, 5 being the highest score.

0–10 The only excuse for a score this low is if you are just starting out. If that is the case, use the criteria as a guideline for the skills you need to master to become a good employee. There are many immediate steps you can programme into your daily routine to help you to fit into the work ethos.

If you scored this low and are not just starting out, take your job more seriously or give up the ghost!

11–25 You have a bit of a way to go before you will make employee of the year. If the skills you fall short in are skills needed for any type of employment, you must make more effort in these areas. Consult with your boss for suggestions on ways to improve on these basic skills and ask for more feedback on your performance.

If you feel your basic skills are fine but your enthusiasm for your current job isn't there, you need to spend some time thinking about what you would rather be doing. Early on in your career you will change jobs a few times before you find one that really clicks. If you can't give a job all your enthusiasm, find a better fit.

26–40 You are a responsible employee and contribute fairly to the company effort. If you are at the higher end of the spectrum, you are career and goal oriented and work well in your current position. If you reached the highest score, you should consider moving on to take on additional responsibilities.

one of the team

To be a successful part of any organization requires you to have the social skills to be able to fit in with the team. You must be able to get on with your co-workers and be able to engage in conversation about work-related issues enabling you to collectively get the work done. This requires flexibility, good listening skills and constructive debate.

Your performance is judged not only on your individual contribution, but also on how effective you are at contributing to group projects and activities. Team players are valued members of all businesses and are at the core of making companies run efficiently. Without everyone working towards a mutual goal, there would be chaos.

Each member of a team has individual strengths and weaknesses. Effective teams utilize each member's strengths to get the job done. It is important to understand what is expected from each team member so if the team leader does not clarify your role, be sure to ask them to write it down.

If you are extrovert and like to speak in groups, you won't find team work a problem. However, if you are an introvert and like to think things out before speaking, you might find a group environment more difficult. The extrovert needs to refrain from dominating the group and the introvert must understand that his/her contribution is important. Each member of the team has specific skills to contribute. The more focussed the team remains on reaching the end result, the less time and effort it will take to get the job done.

Not all teams run smoothly. Personalities can and do clash. However, by following some basic guidelines for your own personal behaviour in team situations, you can stay out of the fray and get your work done.

Be prepared

When meetings go on for ever and take up too much time, it's easy to lose interest. The best way to ensure that meetings stick to schedule is to be sure you are fully prepared to discuss the issues on the agenda and have all the information you require to add your contribution to the group effort.

✖ review agenda and prepare necessary information
✖ distribute information in advance
✖ clarify any questions in advance
✖ contribute at the appropriate time
✖ show respect for time: be on time and don't prolong meetings by speaking too much

Flexibility

Not all projects go according to plan. Rather than pointing the finger of blame, the flexible team player gets on with the next idea to accomplish the mission on hand. If extra work is required, the team player is at it until the job is done.

✖ no complaints when problems arise
✖ easily change direction when required
✖ open-minded attitude towards new ideas
✖ listen respectfully to colleagues' ideas/opinions
✖ accept directions from others
✖ pitch in to help – even if you think the task is beneath you

Compromise

If the common goal is to work towards a resolution, all input is thrown into the equation to reach the desired result. Expanding your viewpoint through a colleague's ideas helps everyone in the team feel part of the solution.

✖ back down from deeply entrenched beliefs
✖ give 100 per cent commitment to consensus
✖ be non-judgemental
✖ do not hold personal grudges

Accept/give constructive criticism

✖ seek evaluation
✖ learn from constructive feedback
✖ don't take things personally
✖ do not be malicious in giving criticism
✖ point out the good before the bad

Appropriate body language

✖ sit up straight
✖ uncrossed arms
✖ don't fidget
✖ eye contact

Acknowledge mistakes

✖ always accept responsibility for mistakes
✖ apologize to anyone hurt as a result
✖ think about how to do it better next time

how well do you play with others?

Using the above skills as the criteria, rate how well you work within a team environment. Rate your skills on a scale of 1–5, 5 being the highest, for each of the categories above. The more practice you get at participating in all types of group activities, the easier it will be for you to realize how your individual contribution can influence the whole. Each group dynamic will be different – personalities and agendas will change – however, by respecting your colleagues' opinions and ideas and adding your individual thoughts, you can be counted on to be a good team player.

Having to perform in front of others can bring out anxieties that may not be present when you work alone. Many of the skills required can be learned with a bit of practice, and some you can take on board instantly.

0–9 Some people are best suited to working alone, and perhaps you're one of them. If you find it difficult not to be the star attraction, you need to find the type of competitive atmosphere where you can push yourself forward. If, however, you want to fit into a bigger organization and your shyness or lack of confidence is a hindrance, there are easy ways to boost your confidence. The personal guidelines that follow on page 142 will help you contribute your fair share.

Ask your team leader for guidance so you can develop the required skills.

10–20 Slight improvements can make a big difference between an average team player and a great one. Review all the skills that need improvement and make a conscious effort to work on them at the next group activity. Make a positive reminder list to help you focus on those points during the meeting. Evaluate how you think you did and how you would do things differently next time. Ask your team leader to evaluate your skills to see if you come across as you think you do.

21–30 You make great efforts to get on with things and do your part for the team. If you really enjoy the dynamics of group activities, you may find managing or leading a group an enjoyable task.

personal guidelines

✖ Get to know everyone on the team.
✖ Understand the mission.
✖ Which of your skills are most needed?
✖ Clarify your role in the team.
✖ Always voice an opinion when you have one.
✖ One speaker at a time – don't interrupt.
✖ Give your undivided attention to whomever is speaking.
✖ Never have side conversations during a meeting.
✖ Make sure phone and other devices are on silent.
✖ Don't criticize the person even if you are critical of the ideas.
✖ Don't take criticism personally.
✖ Don't speak behind someone's back inside or outside the meeting.
✖ Always go to the team leader with any questions/problems.

If you are the team leader

✖ Plan meetings well in advance. Offer several alternatives to ensure everyone can attend.

✖ Send out an agenda as far in advance of the meeting as possible. Invite discussion prior to the meeting.

✖ Schedule the meeting late in the day with a specific time limit. People will work faster when it is the end of the day and they want to get home.

✖ Be sure all team members know each other. Start with introductions and say something nice about each participant.

✖ Clarify the big picture – the overall mission. Everyone needs to buy into the big picture to get the most commitment from the team.

✖ State the goals of the meeting in a specific and measurable way. Set a time limit and exactly what is to be achieved i.e. a one-page summary of action in the next hour.

✖ Assign each individual a specific role in the team. Allow individual input so you know how each team members feels he/she could contribute most.

✖ Clarify the rules. Explain how decisions will be taken and the order of command. Discuss how to communicate with team members in between meetings.

✖ Encourage new ideas. Never judge ideas until the end of the session to spark creativity and group interaction.

✖ Stay neutral. The job of a team leader is to summarize, keep people on track and make sure everyone in the team participates. You need to manage the aggressors and introverts to allow group participation.

✖ Evaluate progress. Allow the team to evaluate their performance and seek ways to improve the dynamics.

when to take the lead

Showing initiative makes you a well-respected employee, for every company demands fresh new ideas. When you feel as though you can contribute more than your current workload demands, ask for additional responsibilities. Letting your immediate supervisor know you want to advance your career or try more challenging tasks will free up their time for more important things. This is the most direct method of working your way up the corporate ladder.

You don't always have to wait for work to be thrown your way. Look at the tasks being done in the office and see if there is anything you feel you can help with or even suggest better ways of doing. Volunteering your services is a sure way to get noticed and will make you a cooperative team player. It's always more fun to be active and engaged at work rather than just sitting around being bored.

Set aside at least three hours a week for your personal work development and use this time to think about new ideas and strategies that can further your company's business goals. Spend time working on an idea for a project that would utilize your skills and present it to your boss. Even if it is not accepted, your boss will know that you are thinking about your job as a career.

When you are able to take charge of a project, be a sensitive manager of people's time and ideas. Be clear about your expectations, timings and always make it a point to praise everyone's contributions. For further guidelines on being in charge, go to page 124 and review the role of a boss and team leader.

office etiquette

Groups of people working together in a confined space need to follow a code of conduct to ensure everyone works to the best of their abilities without interference and distractions from co-workers.

✖ Respect your co-workers' time. Don't call unnecessary meetings or engage in idle conversation as a matter of routine. Get to the point as quickly and concisely as possible.

✖ Respect your co-workers' space. Even if you work in an open-plan office, ask permission before entering a co-worker's personal work area.

✖ Keep your area free from clutter. Your messy desk can make it difficult for your neighbours to concentrate, especially if you make lots of noise when trying to find things. Do not over-personalize your space. You are there to focus on work, not on your personal life.

✖ Always tidy up before leaving a space. If you use a general meeting room, or have a meeting in a co-worker's space, be sure to leave everything neat and tidy. Put chairs back in their place and take all paperwork out with you. If there is cleaning staff, be sure to let them know when you have vacated the space.

✖ If you share equipment, always leave things in good working order. Fill the copier with paper or the fax machine with toner – whatever is required after your use – leave it ready for the next person.

✖ Monitor your speaking level. It's easy to raise your voice in animated conversation, but be sensitive to those around you. Ask your neighbours if they think your voice is too loud and work at speaking in a lower tone. Also remember that it is difficult not to overhear other people's conversations when they are close by.

✖ Turn your personal mobile off during working hours. If you have a work-related mobile, turn to silent/vibrate mode to keep noise levels down.

✖ Never take a call during a meeting. If you are expecting an important call, explain beforehand and excuse yourself when it comes through.

✖ Do not eat strong-smelling or noisy food at your desk. If you do eat at your desk, clear it up immediately you have finished.

✖ If you arrange food for meetings, keep in mind your co-workers' dietary preferences when placing the order. Make sure there is something to suit everyone's tastes.

✖ Do not wear heavy perfumes. Strong-smelling flowers or candles can also cause offence, so ask before introducing them into your workspace.

✖ Dress appropriately. Do not wear clothing that may offend co-workers or members of the public.

✖ Always let at least one of your co-workers know where you are when you are away from your desk.

✖ Always say please and thank you to those around you.

✖ Help out wherever help is needed and you can contribute. If you see a co-worker struggling with something, ask if you can be of service. Sometimes people are too proud to ask and volunteering nicely can make it easier for them to accept help.

the A–Z of best office practice

Action feels good

Be on time

Clear your space at the end of each day

Delegate and let go

Enthusiasm for each task

Flexibility helps you get around obstacles

Goal-setting helps finish tasks more easily

Handle paperwork daily

Investigate all options, but give yourself a time frame

Justify your time

Keep one diary for all facets of your life

Lists help focus the mind

Manageable chunks

No, I can't!

One-minute rule (see page 59)

Plan ahead

Quiet time each day

Reward yourself

Stay seated until completed

Tough stuff first

Use e-mail effectively

Visualize the end result

Write things down in one place

X things off your list when completed for a sense of achievement

You lead by example

Zero in on the important things

working
from your
home office

Whether you chose to work at home to suit your lifestyle or are employed by a company to work outside an office environment, setting up an office and working efficiently from your home base needs to be managed effectively. All the organizational skills you have learned at the office are even more important when you are working from home in order to help distance your personal from your professional life. When the two become one, you are in trouble. At the end of the day, unless you have left your home office in an organized and tidy state, you will never be able to separate the two.

I have worked from my home office for the last nine years and can't imagine having it any other way. After spending thirty years in a variety of company environments, it's nice to have the contrast of the peace and quiet on my own. Working at home requires strong motivational skills and a great degree of self-discipline. No one is looking over your shoulder telling you what you can or cannot do, and there are many distractions that can easily take your focus away from your daily goals. I am very good at substituting a job around the house for a work-related task and never realized how much fun doing the laundry could be until I used it as an excuse to avoid doing some work!

If you are a telecommuter – working as an employee for a company outside the office environment – you will still have some corporate structure to adhere to. So even though you work from home, you are still expected to be present and accounted for during the regular business hours of your company. You will be required to communicate with your boss or colleagues on a regular basis and will probably go into the office at regular intervals for meetings and project updates. On the plus side, you waste less time on commuting and have more time for personal priorities. On the downside, you may not feel as connected to what is going on at the office and worry about being passed over for promotion as your work may not be as obvious as that of co-workers in the office.

Working on your own from home is not for everyone. If you are considering giving up the day job to start your own home business, it's not something to do on a whim. Giving up the benefits of working for a company – health insurance, company pension, paid holidays and sick leave – means you will need financial resources to go it alone. It takes a while for any business to begin generating cash, so if you worry about money, you may want to think twice. You will have to earn at least 30 per cent more than your current salary to make up for the shortfall. You will have to actively promote your business and will perhaps have to be more hands-on than in past positions. Until you can generate enough income to justify the expense of hiring help, you will do it all yourself.

On the other hand, the joys of working from home are numerous. You work in enjoyable, familiar surroundings and can customize your workspace to reflect your personal preferences. You have more flexibility and can dress in a less formal way. I find I can combine my work and household chores into my normal working day and then have time in the evenings to spend with family and friends. If you have children, working from home can give you a bit more time to be with them. However, to run a professional business, your children must not be an interruption to your working day.

I have interviewed many different types of home workers and have reorganized quite a few home offices to make them more pleasant and efficient. The most productive home workers keep regular hours and stick to a daily work routine, beginning and ending at roughly the same time each day. The happiest people had a dedicated office space with comfortable furniture and up-to-date equipment. Many home workers complained of not having enough space to work properly. I also found that people who do jobs in different locations and only required an office to do reports and paperwork, found it more difficult to develop good work habits at home.

Over the years I have developed my own routine that usually helps me accomplish my professional and personal goals. Some days you just have to go with the flow and take time to stop and smell the flowers! Included in this chapter are my secrets for setting up a great home office along with strategies on how to stick to your schedule, stay motivated, use your technology to its best advantage and keep up a professional image while working from home.

home-office essentials

To work successfully from a home-based office, you need the best equipment and the space to put it in. Ideally, you should have a dedicated room that is private and away from family distractions and has the technical capabilities to handle your equipment. If you don't have a spare room, look for the space that fits the following criteria best.

Choosing the best location

We all have different methods of working to capacity. While most people need a private, quiet location with the least distractions, there are people who swear they work best in the middle of the action. The obvious benefit of working from home is that, within the confines of your house, you can choose where best suits your work habits. Keep in mind that when working from home it's not just what is ideal for you – your workspace may also impact on your family. If you need to share space, it's essential that your workspace be cleared up at the end of each day. Look at the following checklist when deciding where to have your office.

✖ electrical outlets
✖ broadband connection/telephone/cable/satellite
✖ good reception for mobile devices
✖ telephone line/business line if warranted
✖ natural light

✖ adequate ventilation

✖ space to spread out

✖ limited distractions

✖ adequate storage

Layout

The ideal home-office layout is U-shaped, providing you with the greatest amount of work surface and storage. Utilize high space for books and office-supplies storage. Low space is ideal for filing. Your chair should be on a sturdy base with good casters and allow you to swivel 360 degrees. Your phone should be within very easy answering distance. If you spend a lot of time on the telephone, a headset is essential.

We discussed the Feng Shui office layout on page 16. The same principles hold true for a home office. At home, however, you can add more ornamentation to your space. Be sure to attract good chi energy with the offer of something lovely at the entrance to your office. My office is in direct line with energy flowing up the stairs from the front door and, to catch it, I have a lovely mosaic table with a big Buddha, fresh flowers, a scented candle and a selection of crystals. I also have a very large jade plant in the rear corner of the office and one on the left corner of my desk.

If you have limited space, work with what you've got. If your office is part of another room, search out a lovely desk that blends in with the decor, but be sure that it will be comfortable to work at. I recently converted a spare room into a guest room and office, and even with limited space you can create a practical and stylish place to work.

No matter where it is located, there needs to be a physical separation from the rest of your home. Bookcases, a screen or large plants can help you keep your mind off work when relaxing.

Zones

The more frequently you use your files or equipment, the closer you position them to your desk. Zone one would include your desk, chair, computer, telephone and anything else you use several times a day. Zone two is overhead or beside your desk and includes things you use at least weekly. Ideally, zone three is behind you and can be easily reached by swivelling around in your chair. This should include reference material, projects not currently being worked on and office supplies you use infrequently.

Equipment
Desk
✖ Minimum 76cm deep.
✖ As much work surface as possible.
✖ Height so elbows are bent at 90 degrees and resting comfortably when seated.

Chair
✖ Padded and comfortable.
✖ Armrests/correct height and width.
✖ Adjustable back.
✖ Adjustable height.
✖ Lumbar support.
✖ Sturdy base.
✖ Appropriate casters for type of floor.
✖ 360 degree swivel ability.

Computer with fast Internet connection

✖ Minimum screen size 38cm – the bigger the better.

✖ Monitor placed at least 50cm from your eyes.

✖ Back-up system/external hard drive.

✖ Flat screen or a monitor arm to save space.

✖ Wireless increases work flexibility.

Good lighting

✖ Overall light free of harsh contrasts and distracting glare.

✖ Desk light for close work.

Business telephone line

✖ Essential, especially if you deal with the general public.

✖ Allows you to advertise your services.

✖ Always answer professionally.

Good-quality printer

✖ Save paper and expensive ink refills by using your printer judiciously. It is easier to scan and e-mail a document than to print things off and post; you save money and the environment.

Fax/scanner/copier

✖ All-in-one machines are fine for occasional use; they take up less space and require fewer power sources. You need something better for lots of reproduction work.

Retrievable voice messaging

✖ An answerphone with a clear message indicating when you are available and how you can be contacted.

Rolling file drawers

✖ Readily available, inexpensive storage option

✖ Enables you to keep files close to hand when working and tucked away when not needed.

✖ Handy way to store office supplies.

Bookshelves

✖ Maximize overhead storage space.

✖ Can be used to divide room.

Amenities

✖ Inspiring and relaxing decor.

✖ Nice window treatments.

✖ Scented candle.

✖ Notice board.

✖ Plants.

✖ Pictures (must show action).

For on the go

✖ BlackBerry.

✖ Laptop computer.

✖ Mobile phone.

✖ Portable printer.

Pay attention to time zones when contacting people abroad and be mindful of interrupting someone's leisure time for something that could wait until tomorrow. When on the phone, give it your undivided attention. The person at the other end of the phone can tell when you are not truly engaged in the conversation. Use common sense when driving and use hands-free equipment.

Ergonomics

The same principles that apply to preventing work-related injuries in the workplace should also apply at home. It's common for people setting up an office from home to try to do it on the cheap, using bits and pieces of old furniture rather than investing in proper kit. In the long run, good furniture is worth the investment. When you feel comfortable and physically well in your space, it's easier to concentrate and be more productive. These are the ergonomic ideals for your equipment.

- **monitor:** top 5cm above eye level, so you look slightly down
- **desk:** elbow height (adjust chair to suit)
- **chair:** feet touching ground or on footrest
- **knees:** hip level or slightly lower
- **elbows:** bent at 60 degrees
- **wrists:** rest on edge of desk – preferably a round edge
- **lower/mid back:** supported

self-discipline and will power

Controlling impulses you know are not in your best interests takes will power. Sticking to a task even though you may not like doing it takes self-discipline. Both will power and self-discipline require you to look towards future gratification from achieving the desired end result.

If you are not naturally self-disciplined or lack will power, you have probably tried to change your habits over the years without much success. We begin each new year making resolutions to improve our lifestyle. Over 90 per cent of us have given up before the first of February. To achieve your goals, you must always look at the long-term advantages of completing them. The other key factor is to make sure your goals are realistic and that deep down you believe you can achieve them. Intending to lose three dress sizes can be an admirable goal, though probably not easily achievable. You must always start small and work up to bigger things. As you begin to reap the benefits of your determination, your will power and self-discipline grow stronger.

Self-discipline is a skill you can learn over time, if you really want to. It requires keeping to a rather strict schedule until your positive new work habits take hold. Begin with a moderate work schedule you can adhere to daily and set small, achievable projects within a given time frame. For example, you decide to work between 10 a.m. and noon each day for a week without interruptions. Build up the set hours and stay put in your office until you achieve what you set out to do. If you can stick to the plan for six weeks you will be well on your way to feeling a sense of accomplishment at the end of each day.

Believe it or not, you can be overly disciplined. Flexibility is a useful trait whether working in a traditional office setting or at home. Some days, for 101 reasons, things just don't go according to plan. On these occasions, break with your traditional routine, get active and do something different. It's important to gain perspective and enjoy the occasions when you can play hooky and have a relaxing day. Distancing yourself from a potential problem can help you come up with new ways to solve it.

Here are some tips to help you stick to your plan:

Don't be polite

I know that sounds funny, but when you work from home it's diffi-cult for some people to take your job seriously. Because you are at home, friends or relatives phone you, pop in or ask you to do favours and chores. Make it clear that you are unavailable during working hours, unless they have scheduled the time in advance and you are happy to take a break. Limit your intake of personal phone calls by choosing a phone that shows incoming numbers.

If you share your home and work when other people are in the house, close your door or put a sign outside that says do not disturb.

Remove yourself from distractions

Always keep in mind that you have complete control of your own actions. If you are trying to diet, don't have fattening foods at home. If you want to give up smoking, you may have to stay away from situations in which you would normally smoke. It's the same with work: it's easier to resist temptation when you stay as far away as possible.

Try to avoid:

✖ computer games and frequent web browsing
✖ music/television
✖ food consumption as procrastination
✖ personal telephone calls during working hours

Make your office inviting

It really helps to have a lovely space to work in, and I must admit my office is one of the nicest rooms in our house. I have two windows looking out onto greenery and a very large built-in desk with lots of surface area. If you enjoy your surroundings and have everything you need at hand to get the job done, your work will seem less of a chore.

Paint your office a colour you find conducive to working in. Shades of yellow are great for will power, green for growth and pale shades of blue can be calming if you are not prone to 'getting blue'. Warm neutrals will be less harsh than bright whites.

Visual cues keep you on track

Writing things down is a great way to help commit them to memory. A large, monthly planner on the wall or door to your office can help keep you focussed on professional and personal commitments and can be a great incentive to get things done. If you can see you have a lovely evening out planned, it's a sure-fire way to help you get on and finish your work by the end of the day. It is also a great way of keeping other household members up to date with your schedule. I suggest a white board that can easily be amended. Colour code your priorities so you can see the important stuff at a glance.

Do routine tasks at the same time every day

Check e-mails first thing in the morning, after lunch and prior to closing up shop for the evening. Try to avoid checking them at all hours of the evening. You need to switch from business to pleasure and give your mind some time to rest.

Go to the post office at the same time each day, so you have a time to work towards. If you plan to send off correspondence by 4.00 it will give you a target to aim for.

Plan mid-morning and mid-afternoon breaks at the start of each day and stick to the schedule. They don't have to be at the same time each day, but they need to be planned at the start of each day. Avoid excessive breaks as an excuse to procrastinate.

Get out of the house often

Without the stimulation of co-workers and travel, it is easy to get tunnel vision about your work. It is extra important to go out and meet new people, generate new business and leads, check out what is going on within your industry and escape from the house. Mental stimulation will increase your creativity and enable you to think of new ideas and ways of doing things.

Increase your will power and self-discipline

Will power and self-discipline are strengthened each time you test them and succeed. It doesn't matter what area of your life you practise your skills in; each time you successfully control your urges to do something you know isn't right, you gain a greater understanding of the power you have to control your actions.

When you try to change any habit, it's always easier to start with the non-emotional things first. There's a big difference between doing a hated chore around the house and giving up nicotine, so I always suggest starting with easy things first. So for the next week:

Get up twenty minutes earlier: Imagine how much more you could get done if you were up and at it twenty minutes earlier. If you have a family to look after, a few minutes to get yourself together first can help you feel more in control of your life and help you get to grips with the day. An extra twenty minutes means you can read the newspaper, have a relaxed breakfast, an extra-long grooming regime or a brisk walk to start your day.

Do a hated household chore as soon as it comes due: Force yourself to deal with it immediately – be it dishes, light bulbs, laundry or whatever. Don't put it off.

I'll do it for five minutes: The hardest part of any task is beginning it. Play the five-minute challenge and see how much you can get done by devoting five minutes of your undivided attention to the task. Push yourself to do another five minutes and if the momentum is with you, keep it going. If not, give it another five minutes in an hour's time.

Give up a small thing you enjoy: Self-discipline is not only about sticking to a task; it's also about duty over pleasure. On many occasions you will have to give things up in order to live up to the commitments you have made. For the next week give up a little pleasure such as the extra coffee/chocolate bar/glass of wine. Just one little thing each day for a week. You can do it.

Stick to a budget: Allocate a certain amount of money you can afford to spend for the week and keep within the budget. Work out all your expenses and how much you have left over to play with. Leave your credit and debit cards at home.

Take a challenge for charity – long term: It's sometimes easier to prove your strength of character when you know you are doing it for a good cause. Signing up for a charity walk or run three to six months in the future is a good reason to stick to your decision and, by raising money, you are undertaking to do your best.

the importance of incentives and rewards

When you were a child, you were probably told you couldn't have your pudding until you finished your first course. If you really wanted the pudding, it was a good enough incentive to eat the things you didn't like or want. If the pudding wasn't to your liking, you probably ended up in your room for refusing to finish your meal. You learn from an early age to work towards incentives you like and want.

Every day there will be a few things to do you don't like doing. In the grand scale of life, they won't take very much time once you make the effort, but, oh, how much time you can waste thinking about ways to avoid doing them. Planning a treat when you have completed a task will give you the motivation to do it. The treat has to be something you really want, even if it is something small. The more you associate finishing things up with getting rewards the more it will help you keep on track.

In the big picture, you work towards an overall quality of life that meets your dreams and ambitions. The more clearly you can keep your long-term goals in mind, the easier you will find putting in the hours and effort to get there. The more specific the goal, the more in control you are of achieving it. Keep visual cues accessible to remind you what you are aiming for – a picture of your favourite holiday spot, or a house you would like to live in. Whatever you want, try to see it as clearly as you can.

When you work on your own, you don't get the same pats on the back you would get in a larger organization. Providing your own acknowledgement of successfully completing your tasks will make it easy to tackle them in the future. If you think something nice will happen when you get to the end of a time limit, it makes you want to get there more quickly. Here are a few motivational reward techniques you can try each day.

Make a list of quick treats

Whenever you finish a two-hour segment of work or complete a small task, award yourself fifteen minutes of responsible fun. Make a list right now of things that would uplift you and make you feel good, without overindulging to compensate for working hard. In other words, a small piece of chocolate is good – a pint of ice cream, bad. Consider a walk around the block, quick nap in the garden or a fix of your favourite music or a nice cup of tea.

Celebrate your big successes

Whenever you exceed your expectations, or achieve a goal on time, share your success with those you love. When you say things out loud, you accept your success and indicate you want more. You don't have to be boastful to be proud of your achievements.

Learning from your success will help you continue to improve. Reflect upon the qualities you exhibited that enabled you to achieve your goals. Examine the hours you worked, times of the day you were most productive and the type of work you found interesting.

Each experience enables you to hone your preferences to find the best work schedule for you.

Plan big events at least three months in advance

Forward planning enables you to build up the excitement level over time. Booking a holiday in the middle of November for the gloomy month of February is a great example of good planning which provides an incentive. If, between the time you book and the time you go, you need a bit of a boost, do a bit more research into where you are going. Get on the web or buy a travel guide. The anticipation will help you focus on getting your work done.

What benefits do you get from completing each task?

Every time you begin a new segment of your day and start a new task, take a minute or two to write down the benefits you will get when you are done. I would consider the following:

- ✖ paid upon completion
- ✖ closed a file
- ✖ can start something new
- ✖ learned something new
- ✖ recognition
- ✖ self-confidence

Creative visualization

Any time you need an incentive, you can create it in your mind. Use your imagination to motivate you to complete a job and find easy ways to help you do it. When you are in a relaxed state ideas flow more easily. Honest to goodness, it really works. In this exercise you are going to visualize your favourite getaway; I've used mine as an example. Keep in mind that some people are more visual than others, and can see things more clearly in their mind's eye. It doesn't matter whether you can see it clearly, through a haze or not at all.

Imagine it is a lovely summer's day, not too hot and not too cool. The sky is a beautiful shade of blue with a few fluffy white clouds providing the occasional shadows.

You are sitting in a lovely office in a home you don't recognize. The desk is just the right size for you and the chair you are sitting in is a perfect fit. To the left of the desk is a window overlooking a sun-drenched terrace with a view to the village beyond. The window is open and you can smell the jasmine as the curtains ruffle with the occasional breeze. You think about how nice it would be to be outdoors enjoying the glorious day.

You know there is one thing you would really like to get done, and if you can get it done quickly you will be able to go out and make the most of the day. OK, you think, what would be the easiest and quickest way to get this chore out of the way? You begin to make a list of all the ways to do your task quickly. You give yourself one minute to think and make a mental note of the ideas you come up with.

Bring your awareness to the present moment. Wriggle your toes. Write down your ideas and spend the next hour implementing them. Take a break when the hour is up.

tricks of the trade

✖ Dress smartly, even if it's casual. It helps put you into a professional mindset and lets people know you take your job seriously.

✖ Leave your house each morning for a cup of coffee or a quick walk. It helps to separate your home mode from your work mode.

✖ Start each day at roughly the same time. It's better to knock off early than to start late.

✖ Let everyone know where you are and how you can be reached. This can be done on a voice messaging service or through an e-mail message.

✖ If you are away from your office, check for messages frequently if you are expecting people to get in touch.

✖ Set strict time limits for each task.

✖ Get help where you need it. Hire a childminder, cleaner, dog walkers. Get part-time help to do things that are not time efficient for you to do such as tax preparation, etc.

✖ Keep good records. Home offices are tax deductible providing they are used exclusively for business use. Check with your tax officer or accountant to find out the requirements. Keep all receipts in one place – a clearly marked envelope kept in a prominent location.

✖ Use Instant Messaging on your computer if you want a quick live-time chat.

✖ No time is too little to do a little bit. If you think of an idea and don't have much time, just take a few minutes to write it down. A short time doing something when you think of it can save hours trying to remember what it was you wanted to do.

✖ Keep your desk neat and tidy and put everything away in its place at the end of the day.

✖ Start each day raring to go and aim to finish early.

✖ Plan several early days a week so you can prepare dinner or go out for the evening.

✖ Always have a bit of ice cream in the freezer!

can you have it all?

understanding work/life balance

The simple answer to the question 'Can I have it all?' is no. As hard as you try, it is near impossible to strike the perfect balance between professional and personal life goals. Subscribing to the myth that it *is* possible will leave you feeling a failure a good deal of the time and will drive you and those around you crazy in the process! Trust me – I know this from personal experience.

The truth is that at some times in your life, the balance between work and a personal life is unattainable and there will be something you have to give up in order to achieve some of your goals. The question is whether it will be worth the sacrifice in the long run, and that is a question only you can answer.

When you think about work/life balance, most people imagine that it is a 50/50 split. You spend half your time at work and the remainder doing the personal things that are important to you to have a fulfilled life. In the long-term, this balance works out – you will spend about half your life working to achieve the financial and personal success you desire, but at different stages of your life the work/personal balance will be out of kilter to accommodate those very things you want.

The thing about a work/life balance is that it constantly shifts over time. At the beginning of your working life, the balance is probably more towards the personal side of your life. Entry-level positions rarely provide the financial motivation or mental stimulation to keep you focussed on the job. The desire for a home, partner or children will make the balance shift – you may need to work more to support your financial commitments or want to take time off to start a family. Money is a strong motivating factor for working the hours required to be a success. Towards the end of your career, you might work even harder as younger competition threatens your position and you feel you have to make the effort while you are still able to rise to the challenge.

If you are a woman, you have the added pressure of deciding if and when to have children. The ticking of your biological clock adds increased pressure the older you get. If you want a successful career and a family there will inevitably be some rocky times ahead. The feelings of guilt and anxiety at leaving your children at home to go back to work can wreak havoc on your mental outlook and trying to be perfect at both can make your life hell. You will have to work harder at your job to prove your commitment, leaving less time to get everything done.

In addition, the boundaries between work and personal lives have changed beyond all recognition, especially with advanced technology and the globalization of world markets. Businesses operate

24/7 and there is increasing pressure to work longer hours to be successful in the fast pace of today's world. Even if you aren't in the office, your ability to be contacted anywhere at any time can make it difficult to dedicate time solely to your personal affairs.

At some stage of your life I believe you can have everything you want all at the same time. To be successful at anything takes hard work. Whether you have a natural talent or an acquired skill, you will need to work at it constantly to develop your full potential. You will also need to give it your undivided attention. To be successful in your work and personal life you must give each one time and attention. The amount of time doesn't matter, as long as in the time you have, you give it your all. Your work life can and should be exhilarating and the desire to contribute something to the world is an overwhelming natural urge. If sometimes it means your personal life suffers, I believe that with good communication skills and by making the most of the personal time you do have, you and your family can weather the storm and achieve an equilibrium that is satisfying to all.

are you happy?

Who's to say what a balanced life is? Your mother, for example, would have one definition that would surely differ from your own. Your values, the things that are the most important to you, will define your idea of balance, and as long as your values and your partner's values, if you have a family, are in synch, how many hours you spend at work isn't the issue.

What life is really about is being happy. If you get your thrills by working twelve hours a day, good on you. That's pretty much all that matters, as long as you look after your health in the process. If you spend the same twelve hours at work miserable and unhappy, you will obviously feel you are giving up too much to make it worth your while. It's then time to take active steps to re-assess your goals and re-think your job.

Take this work/life challenge to assess how you feel about the balance in your life right now in the moment. Rate each statement on the following scale:

1 – never
2 – rarely
3 – sometimes
4 – most of the time
5 – always

✖ I work all the hours my job requires.
✖ I feel I get my work done by the end of the day.
✖ I can leave my work at the office.
✖ I can leave my personal life at home.
✖ I spend enough time with my partner/family.
✖ I see my friends on a regular basis.
✖ I have time to do the chores around the house.
✖ I have time to eat properly.
✖ I have time to look after my personal grooming.
✖ I have time to look after my physical fitness.
✖ I have time for relaxation.
✖ I take all the holiday time allowed me.
✖ I get help where I can to do routine things that time won't allow.

13–30 Unless there is a physical or emotional reason that you have scored so low, you are seriously lacking in good organizational skills. Either you have aimed too high and are out of your league, or haven't found the self-discipline to be able to start and finish. You need to re-think your job and assess the things that motivate you. Review chapter 2 on page 45.

31–43 In that you generally do OK at fitting things in, review your answers to see what particular areas need improvement. If you gave yourself a middle of the road score on most things, try tackling them with more concentration and dedicated effort. You're almost achieving the balance, but not quite to a standard of excellence. You may find you get higher ratings for one part of your life over the other. Use the same focus and dedication on the weaker area as you do on your stronger areas. More focus does not have to mean more time.

44–59 Good going. This score shows an overall balance of duty and pleasure and a flexible personality. It's not about getting it right all the time, or life would be plain boring. You continue to learn and improve by keeping up the effort and gain the rewards by enjoying the benefit of your hard work. This is the ultimate reward.

60–65 I always worry a little about perfection. The need to get every detail correct can lead to many emotional problems and troubled relationships. You must accept your humanity and relax a bit to take things in.

There are, of course, always things you can do to improve upon the amount of personal time you manage to have. All the time-management skills you have practised throughout the book will help you get more work done in less time. Blocking out realistic personal time off and planning memorable activities during this time can help you learn to shift the focus from work to personal with the same degree of attention. Small things go a long way in helping to realize a better quality of life. You can also learn to let go of the unimportant. The world won't come to an end if your bed isn't made every day, you can't cook a meal or there are a few cobwebs on the ceiling. It's all a matter of priorities.

If you feel your life is out of balance and one part is suffering, don't despair. Try to keep in mind that, in time, things will change. If patience is not one of your virtues, by all means take active steps to feel more in control of how you would like your life to be. I hope the following strategies can help you work out the balance more effectively.

define your short-term goals

When something has a beginning and an end, you can plan efficiently for it and see yourself completing it – the two main ingredients in helping you achieve a successful outcome. It's easier to plan for short-term things as your reward will come more quickly. In the process of trying to achieve this short-term goal you may have to work harder and give up some things in the process. I think most people can tolerate just about anything if they can see an end in sight. If you have ever had builders in your house for any length of time you will be able to relate to this!

Short-term goals can be anything – from a daily task to something you would like to achieve within the next three to six months, for example. It helps to set a time limit on the goal so you challenge yourself creatively for ways to accomplish it on time. The more time you have, the more time you are likely to take. Be realistic but challenging to provide the greatest motivation.

Think thirty days ahead

For the purpose of this exercise, let's focus on picking out a few things to work towards in both your work and personal life over the next thirty-day period. I have listed some ideas you can consider, but the list should be personal to you.

✖ List one project you would like to complete at work.
✖ List one special event you would like to attend.
✖ List one thing you would like to complete at home.
✖ List one person you would like to catch up with.
✖ List one book you would like to read.
✖ List anything else you would like to achieve in the next thirty days.

Consider the possibility that to achieve these goals, you may have to give up doing something else. What things might you have to give up to achieve them? Can you find ways to save time and fit everything in? Can you give up the unimportant? Is the goal worth the sacrifice?

Think three to six months ahead

These will be bigger and more important than your thirty-day goals. Three to six months give you adequate time to put a plan in motion and work towards achieving it. What big things have you put off doing simply because you haven't given the time or effort to working out how to get them done?

Here are some short-term goals to think about, but the list is meant to be personal, so add your individual goals.

✖ pay rise/promotion
✖ change of job
✖ change of living accommodation
✖ change in relationship
✖ plan a holiday
✖ get finances in order
✖ lose two to five kilos
✖ make a major purchase

For each goal you have on your list, write in your diary the date by which you hope to achieve it, then spend two minutes thinking about all the things you will need to put into action to reach your deadline and write them down. Arrange them into daily/weekly/monthly actions that need to be taken and put them in your schedule. Make a one-word reminder for each item on your list to provide a visual cue to keep you on track. Look at the implications each time commitment will have on your current schedule. Think about what you might have to give up to achieve your goals.

long-term goals

Thinking about the future is a responsible thing to do. Good financial planning when you are young will help alleviate a lot of stress and worry in your later working years about whether you will have enough money to enjoy life in retirement. Defining your long-term goals will give you an understanding of how much money you need to tuck away over the years to achieve them, which will go a long way in providing the incentive and motivation to work as hard as you must to earn it.

As life always brings many surprises, your long-term goals may completely shift over time. What you thought you wanted at twenty will surely differ from what you want at forty, so your long-term goals are flexible and subject to change. Each new life experience helps more clearly to define your preferences. If you stick rigidly to a plan you may miss out on more exciting opportunities. It's good to do the occasional reality check to see if what you always thought you wanted is what you still want today.

In order to achieve long-term goals, you must incorporate them into your daily life. It's great to have an ideal picture in your mind of where you would like to be in five, ten and even twenty years' time, but remember, in order to achieve that picture you have to take daily action to get there. When you think about these goals every day, it strengthens your connection to them and enables you to see how well you are doing towards getting there.

It can be difficult to think about what you want to do when you retire and although you will need adequate financial resources to be able to take it easier and enjoy life more, when you are twenty-five, retirement may seem a very long way away. Approaching long-term goals by looking at where you want to be in five or ten years' time can make them easier to imagine, and therefore easier to achieve. As you reach your first set of longer-term goals, move the goal posts and look towards the next five-year segment.

It is important to set your goals in a positive way. Rather than saying, 'In five years I don't want to be stuck in this dead end job', say, 'In five years I would like to be working for a company where I can manage a staff and earn in the range of x–y salary a year.' You can break this positive goal down into achievable daily action steps to help you get there. The closer you get towards achieving your goal, the easier it is to find the energy and commitment to push onwards.

The key to any goal setting is to make it specific, measurable, with a specific time frame and positive.

To help define your long-term goals, ask yourself the following questions:

✖ If money weren't an obstacle, what would I be doing with my life?

✖ Where would I like to live?

✖ What would I do with my time?

✖ Do I want to have a family?

✖ What material things would I like to own?

✖ Where would I like to travel?

Answering these questions helps stimulate your imagination and gives you a visual idea of your life goals. The more clearly you can picture the things you want to do the easier it is to stay connected to the vision you are working towards on a daily basis.

Looking at the things you want, test your maths skills by roughly figuring out how much it would cost to have them. Work it out in today's costs and, once you set a time frame for it, you can add additional sums for inflation. For example, if you want to have a house in a specific area, look at how much the house costs today. If you think you can achieve this in five years' time, think about how much the house will cost then and add this amount to the equation.

Now look at each goal and see when you realistically think you could achieve it. Place a rough date next to each goal. You now know how much it costs and how long you have to save the amount of money required to achieve it.

Once again using your creative side, without judging the answers, write down twenty-five ways you could earn the money to achieve each goal. Give yourself three minutes per goal and write down anything that comes to mind, realistic or not – don't judge. When you have finished, go through the list and number them, starting with the easiest and most practical one first. Break each step down into manageable chunks and incorporate them into your daily plans.

give up the unimportant

When you try to fit everything in, something's got to give, and it is usually the personal time you require for sleep and relaxation. In order for your body to work efficiently, you need to nourish it with good food and give it down time to regenerate. Rushing around trying to attend to every detail at work, home and in your personal relationships is exhausting.

Setting priorities and relaxing the standards are two ways to gain personal time. On many occasions, good is good enough. Sometimes, in striving to get something perfect, you overdo your efforts when less would have sufficed. Producing a 100-page report when fifty would do, will not necessarily gain you credit. Efficiency is about being able to judge what is most important in each task you undertake.

Learning to accept that everything can't be perfect all the time is a good life lesson. Sometimes you just have to ignore things you would like to do but can't, and remember that, although you can't do them now, you will be able to do them some time in the future. Letting go of things that really don't matter in the grand scheme of life will immediately take a lot of weight from your shoulders.

Have a look at some of the routine tasks you can give up or do with less frequency in your work and personal life in order to gain time for yourself. Pass on tasks at work, if possible, to someone who wants added responsibility. Look at the cost-benefit analysis of hiring help to do the household chores that eat into your personal time.

Work-related tasks
* telephone
* correspondence
* filing/admin
* initial review of reports/documents
* expense reports
* travel arrangements
* committees

Home-related tasks
* cleaning
* bill paying/taxes
* cooking
* shopping

✖ laundry
✖ child care
✖ maintenance
✖ garden
✖ pet care

Also look at ways you can relax your standards in completing the above tasks. If you can't make your bed in the morning or don't have time to prepare a three-course meal, go for the easier option. Let the bed go undone and have a bowl of cereal for dinner – as long as it is not for ever, you can live with the consequences. Look at some of the areas where your perfectionism takes up too much time and do each task for less time.

don't feel bound by traditional roles

Traditional family roles are changing as both men and women can now have highly paid executive positions. What was once considered the sole burden of the female member of the household should be up for grabs. Housework and childcare are equal opportunity employers.

Many women still operate in the belief, or in many cases, the reality, that they are expected to maintain the home as well as go to work. Although the traditional family has changed greatly over the years through divorce, gay marriage and single parenthood, it's hard to erase the old working model as we begin the twenty-first century. I'm sure that much marital strife is predicated on an unequal balance of household responsibilities between partners. The trouble with expecting something to be done is that you rarely appreciate the effort it took to do it.

If you feel there is a gender imbalance in the tasks required to make your life run efficiently and happily for everyone involved, it helps to address the problems. There are several approaches to take. In both cases, start with a list of all of the non-work-related chores and responsibilities and how often they need doing. Both partners should have a diary to hand in this planning process.

Who's best at what?

A sensible approach to take is playing to each other's strengths. If one of you is a great cook and enjoys cooking, they should take that job. However, in order for each of you to appreciate the effort involved in a particular task, reverse roles at least twice a month. It is nice to have a break and to understand the process.

If you have children, by all means involve them in each of the chores in a small way so they understand what it takes to keep a household running efficiently. Be sure both boys and girls do all tasks.

Shared responsibilities

The second approach is a rota system where you each take turns at doing all the chores for a period of time. If you both hate housework, it's a fair system to share the burdens! Draw up a thirty-day rota at the beginning of each month and hang it up where everyone can see what is expected of them. The kitchen is usually the place where everyone congregates. Keep it simple and clear with the person's name, their chores and the days those chores need doing. By sticking to a plan over four weeks you can develop it as part of your routine. Changing it on a weekly basis will waste time and lead to confusion.

make the most of the personal time you have

It's never about the amount of free time you have, but rather what you do with it. Giving your personal time the same amount of planning and attention to detail that you would your business matters means you will gain the maximum benefit from your time off. Even something as simple as catching up on your sleep will benefit from good planning. Imagine getting into a freshly made bed, flowers by your side, a breeze coming through an open window – bliss! To achieve this takes planning.

There are some events that should always take priority such as birthdays and anniversaries. Most of these can be scheduled in advance, so always try your best to stick to these plans. If you know

acceptance

When things are out of kilter and don't go according to plan, learn to accept and let go. Holding on to the anger or self-defeating notions of failure will help further create an imbalance in your life.

Laugh at your mistakes and the circumstances that have created a day not to your liking, and accept that you learn more about yourself from these experiences than when everything goes to plan. Share your mistakes with someone you love and see how easily they float away.

Do something to make yourself feel better. Watch a funny movie, listen, or better yet, sing to music, have a glass of wine or indulge in a treat. Tomorrow is another day!

you won't be able to, say so beforehand and plan a time close to the event when you know you will be able to celebrate. It's better to be truthful than to let someone down.

Take a look at some ways you can plan some special time for yourself with your family or friends. Rather than scheduling unrealistic things in your diary like dinner out once a week, save up the pleasure and make it more special. Plan an exceptional dinner out once a fortnight and really make it magic.

In the next month, plan a special day out or an event to cover the following areas of your life.

✖ day of shopping
✖ day of grooming
✖ day with partner/friends
✖ day with family
✖ cultural event
✖ outdoor event
✖ intellectual activity
✖ relaxing at home

letting go of emotional baggage

Emotional baggage keeps you stuck in the past. Whether it is holding on to the physical reminders of unhappy events, or holding on to the emotions/feelings attached to those events, until you release them, it will be difficult to allow new, happier experiences to enter your life. You will spend excessive time worrying rather than focussing on making new things happen.

During the course of your life you will:

✖ fail at some things

✖ lose someone close to you

✖ make lots of mistakes

✖ be hurt by someone

✖ be overly sensitive to something

✖ be laughed at

✖ get depressed

I like to look at each thing as a mini life lesson, gain from the experience and move on. I have personally experienced each item on the list on many, many occasions and have survived to create new things. Each negative experience can stop you dead in your tracks if you let it, but learning something new from the experience and gaining a deeper understanding of your personal strengths and weaknesses can help you forge ahead as a more experienced individual.

Time is a great healer

Each of us will handle loss, failure, or the fact that we are not perfect in different ways and within different time frames. Some people can let things go like water off a duck's back, while others remain stuck in quicksand, being dragged down by the weight of the experience for long periods of time.

Perspective and positive thinking can help you turn things around. Even when you experience a personal loss, looking at the positive and wonderful things a person or experience had in your life, feels much better than focussing on what you no longer have. Life is filled with contrasts to enable you to appreciate and experience the good things daily. If each and every day were the same, life would be extremely boring. You need contrast to help you choose what you want.

Think about something you think you failed at some time in the last year or two. Hopefully, it will be an experience you have moved on from. Re-create the experience in your mind's eye and try to remember how you felt. With the benefit of time, what have you learnt from that failure? Please add your particular lessons to the list below.

✖ wasn't thought to be a failure by my colleagues
✖ Something I didn't enjoy doing
✖ Something I procrastinated about and didn't give my best effort to
✖ Didn't fully understand what was expected of me
✖ Wasn't working in the right environment/right position

Ask yourself the following questions:

✖ Have you changed your approach and learned from the experience?
✖ How have you incorporated what you learned into your daily routine?
✖ Given the benefit of hindsight, how would you have done things differently?
✖ Was it as bad as you thought?

Letting go of the past

For each experience you are holding on to and wish to let go of:

✖ Get rid of the material objects associated with the experience where you are able.

✖ Make a list of three experiences you are ready to release.

✖ Beginning with the least emotional experience, follow the visualization below for each experience.

Sit comfortably in a chair, feet on the ground. Close your eyes and take some deep breaths in and out to the count of three. When you are relaxed, bring into your mind a memory that makes you unhappy and you are ready to let go of. Think about where in your body you experience this bad memory. Imagine an opening appears in the part of your body where you feel the negative experience. It is bursting to get out towards the light where it can be released and turned into positive energy. For each negative experience you are ready to let go, allow the feelings to be released. Each time you let one go, you begin to feel lighter and more energetic. You can feel a warm glow in the area that has been newly energized and you are ready to move on. When you are finished, you feel happy, content and energetic. Slowly begin to move your limbs about and, in your own time, open your eyes.

moving on

how and when to make a positive job change

At some point in your working life you are likely to change your job. No matter what the circumstances surrounding your decision to leave, there is always some stress involved, especially when you have to tell your boss. If you are looking for a new job while still at your old one, the sneaking around going to interviews can make you feel guilty as well. Leaving your job is nothing to take lightly, so it's important you give it lots of thought and be sure you are doing it for the right reasons.

There are many valid reasons to move on and if you have been contemplating a move for a long time, you probably have had enough. Boredom, lack of appreciation, working in an unpleasant environment that is unlikely to change, becoming physically or emotionally unwell as a result of stress, or a change in your personal circumstances are the most common reasons for leaving a job, along with better offers from another company. It is a good idea to remain in your job for a minimum of two years – it shows commitment and effort and is a good time frame within which to achieve some of your medium-term goals.

In most cases it is better to have another job in place before resigning, but if circumstances are intolerable, do it when you must. It's always easier to plan a move rather than feel you are forced to do it to escape. Planning helps you look towards the future – escape dwells on the negative and the past. It's helpful to save up at least six months' worth of salary before leaving because the combination of financial stress coupled with the stress of finding another job is difficult to handle.

If, however, you have changed jobs often or do it on a whim, you may not have thought about the ramifications. Some people do think that the grass is always greener somewhere else and hop from job to job trying to find the perfect one. In the long run, the more often you switch jobs, the less reliable you become as an employee. If you always find problems everywhere you go, chances are you are creating the chaos as an excuse to move on. Sticking to a job for as long as it takes for you to master it will give you the confidence you need to stay put. Either that, or strike out on your own.

Throughout this book we have explored ways of turning negative habits and situations around. Remembering what you wanted from your present job is an exercise we practised in chapter 3 on page 69. If you haven't achieved all your goals, trying to resolve your work-related problems before deciding to quit will leave you satisfied you made your best effort. I always believe that if you can give something a time frame and try your hardest in that time – sixty days is a good place to start – you can turn things around.

one last go

Changing your attitude towards your job and your colleagues can significantly improve the way you feel and what you are able to accomplish at work. Being proactive always feels better than doing the same thing each day and feeling trapped in a rut. If you haven't achieved what you had hoped in this job, explore the reasons why before you leave. It will help you formulate more realistic goals for future jobs.

There are ways to circumnavigate most problems and giving up may lessen your self-confidence. When you can, sticking things out builds character and helps you learn to deal with the many tough situations life will throw your way. Even committing as few as thirty days of your best efforts towards resolving your work-related issues can help you achieve a successful conclusion, whether you choose to stay or not.

Follow the strategies outlined below for the next thirty days, for the work-related difficulties specific to you. At the end of the month, re-evaluate your position to see if your attitude towards your job has changed. If you have given it your best effort and had no joy, plan your next move.

Physical health

If your work is making you ill, you must get to grips with the root of the problem. It's very difficult to ignore physical pain as it is always in your conscious mind. Physical work-related illnesses such as RSI, sight-related problems or injuries from accidents, can be caused by poor working conditions. You should be able to solve these by speaking to the management of your company. There are workforce rules and regulations, and companies can be subject to fines for not adhering to them. If you can't get it solved, you may have cause for legal action.

Physical illness is also caused by work-related stress. Elevated blood pressure, headaches, asthma or stomach disorders can be symptoms of emotional issues at work. When the thought of going to work triggers these symptoms, it's difficult to get motivated to start your day. It's best to try to beat it, rather than caving in. All jobs have stressful aspects and learning to cope with stress is an important skill to develop.

Physical activity will improve many aspects of your health as well as positively impact on your mental outlook. If you haven't exercised in a long time, start off gently and build up gradually each day. If you have any concerns about your health and exercising, get in touch with your doctor.

Over the next thirty-day period, begin your work day with a physical-fitness routine.

✖ Get up half an hour earlier and have a brisk walk or a run before you get ready for work.
✖ Go to a gym class or have a swim on the way to work.
✖ Walk all or part way to work, rather than taking your car or public transport.

At the start of this thirty-day period there are several little things to do.

✖ Write down five ways you would like to feel physically better – frame them positively. For example, I want to feel clear-headed or breathe more easily.

✖ Take a picture of yourself on the day you begin. Note your weight and current physical condition on the back of the picture and put it in the back of your diary. Don't look at it until the thirty days are up.

✖ Mark out an hour in your diary each day for exercise.

Think about your five goals each time you begin your physical-exercise routine. Challenge yourself to improve a bit more each day by working harder and doing it more quickly when appropriate. At the end of thirty days, check your progress.

✖ Has your physical condition improved?

✖ Did you meet your goals?

✖ Do you feel better mentally?

✖ Do you feel more in control of your situation at work?

Meditation

Another way to reduce stress is to practise meditation. Although it is often associated with mystical or religious practices, it's really a simple relaxation technique that doesn't require much training and can be done for a few minutes to help you clear your mind. Best practice is to try to meditate twice a day – first thing in the morning and last thing in the evening for twenty minutes each session. A little meditation is better than none at all and it can improve the symptoms of stress.

Close your eyes and practise the breathing techniques used on page 36, by sitting comfortably in a chair with your back fully supported and both your feet on the ground. As you begin to feel relaxed, repeat the word ONE in your head until you begin to feel still, peaceful and relaxed. When a thought comes to mind, let it drift away on a fluffy cloud until you are ready to deal with it later. Bring your focus back to the number ONE and allow the state of deep relaxation to occur.

You can play gentle music in the background that is timed to finish when your meditation is complete or set an alarm to remind you of the time. Slowly bring your attention to the present moment by wiggling your feet and shaking your hands. Open your eyes when you feel ready.

Bullying boss

One of the most difficult workplace issues to cope with is the bullying boss and in my experience there are many of them out there. Bullying is not gender specific – both male and female bosses can and do exhibit aggressive behaviour in the workplace, and if your boss bullies you, in all probability he/she has bullied your co-workers as well. It's not pleasant to be humiliated in public, however if it happens to everyone it can make it easier to de-personalize the abuse.

Unfortunately, aggressive behaviour is often viewed as a positive trait in corporate life, especially if it delivers results. Studies show that bullying has no negative impact on work production, so top management is rarely aware of the problem. Few employees are willing to risk their jobs by complaining to the boss's boss, especially when you have to face your boss after you have done it. The only effective way to try that approach is to have everyone in the department join in the complaint at the same time and I wouldn't hold my breath on that happening. In all offices there will be some colleagues who hope to benefit from someone's misfortune.

All that aside, no one says life is fair or that everyone you meet is going to be pleasant. Personally, I think it is worth developing skills to cope with difficult individuals. You may not choose to remain around them for a long time, but if there is still something to be gained from your current job, it's worthwhile toughening up and learning to let things pass. Unfortunately when figures of authority make you feel bad, it can bring up unhappy childhood associations and it's easy to crumble.

These strategies should help you weather the emotional storms:

Pay attention to your boss's habits: Over the next week, see if you can work out a pattern to your boss's habits and moods. Approaching difficult people at just the right time will make a difference in how they react. You can plan accordingly to give you the greatest chance of an easy ride. Quietly observe and note the following:

- What is your boss's mood first thing in the morning?
- How much coffee does your boss drink?
- What does your boss like to eat?
- When does your boss go to lunch?
- What is your boss's mood before and after lunch?
- Does your boss have a snack in the afternoon?
- What time does your boss leave the office?
- Does your boss have a partner or family?
- Are there particular colleagues your boss picks on?
- What makes your boss cross?
- Are there days that are worse than others?

✖ How does your boss interact with his/her boss?

Forearmed is forewarned. Use this intelligence to your best advantage. Never underestimate the benefits of de-caffeinated coffee on a hyperactive boss.

Reinforce positive behaviour in your boss: As impossible as it may seem to find good characteristics in a bullying boss, they must be hiding there somewhere. In most cases, your boss got to be in a position of power by demonstrating successful skills in some area, although not necessarily through his/her people skills. Looking for the positive skills you can learn will make for a better working relationship. Demonstrating your ability to recognize their talents can help them recognize yours. It's worth giving it a go. Sit down and make a list of all the positive talents your boss possesses. What can you learn?

Removing your attention from the negative to focus on the positive is a great life skill in all situations. By reinforcing positive behaviour with praise and ignoring the negative behaviour, the attention seeker will adapt behaviour to gain praise. I am not suggesting you suck up to your boss, just that you praise positive behaviour when it comes your way.

Be sure to smile and be charming when your boss does the following:

✖ acknowledges your existence in a friendly way
✖ gives you clear and concise information
✖ gives you ample time to prepare work
✖ allows you to voice your opinion without criticism

✖ discusses problems behind closed doors
✖ acknowledges your contribution

Ignore:

✖ random outbursts
✖ negative comments about colleagues
✖ attacks on performance

Confrontation

If you are really ready to leave your job and have nothing to lose, standing up to a bully can work, but if it doesn't, there's no chance of remaining in the company. Sometimes people with tough behaviour respect other people with tough behaviour, as long as they are not perceived as a threat. If you are ready to give it a go, here are some tips to help you prepare:

✖ always seek a meeting and have your conversation in private
✖ be specific about incidents and behaviour but don't analyse it
✖ speak in the first person
✖ look your boss in the eye
✖ point out how leadership style affects others in the office
✖ keep emotion out of it

Boredom

There are two types of boredom to consider – boredom with your job within the company or boredom with your profession in general. I'll deal with the second one first. If it's boredom with the profession that is at the root of the problem, there's no pressing reason to leave other than for mental stimulation. Boredom is never a reason to do anything rash. Use the desire to find something new and exciting to plan properly for a new career. Getting excited about something else may even re-kindle your interest in what you are doing – passion and excitement is a powerful force.

You always need new challenges to keep your mind fit, so if you really can't find them at what you are doing now, answer the following questions:

✖ What other skills and talents do you have?
✖ What have you always wanted to do but never tried?
✖ Would you need to learn new skills to do it?
✖ What can you see yourself doing for the remainder of your working career?
✖ Do you have the financial resources to live without working for the time training would take?
✖ Could you make other parts of your life more exciting to compensate for the lack of it at work?
✖ When would you like to be in a new job?
✖ How would you go about finding it?

Review your answers and give yourself thirty days to investigate your feelings and options. Seek advice from at least three professional or personal friends or family members and keep your eyes open for what is out there. Spend an hour a day on the project and at the end of thirty days, review your course of action. Take the steps listed below to hunt down the ideal career to suit your temperament and talents, or be thankful for what you have and put more effort into creating the stimulation you need as explored below. If you are bored with your particular job, you don't have enough stimulation. You may have been doing the same thing for a long time and be ready to do more. If you are bored, it is entirely up to you to take the initiative to take on a more challenging role. Here are some easy things to do to become more engaged in your job:

✖ Look for activities in your department you can voluntarily help with.

✖ Seek out training courses to expand your skills.

✖ Talk to your supervisor to see if there are other jobs available within your department.

✖ Look for a new job in a different department of the same company.

✖ Review your job goals to see if you have attained them. If so, set new challenges and plan a move.

the hunt for a new job

When you decide to change jobs, it pays to be organized. In that your job search overlaps with your current job, you need to be discreet and stay focussed on your work as well as on your personal objectives. Try to spend an hour a day on a focussed work search.

What have you learned?

A great way to think about starting to look for a new job and a fantastic basis for a new CV is to think about all the skills you have acquired in your present position. Looking at your achievements can help you look back favourably on the experience.

✖ How did the skills you learned measure up to the goals you had?

✖ Were there things you thought you would do but didn't?

✖ Did you learn more than your job description required?

✖ What new skills will you take with you to a new position?

Once you have listed all your skills, think about the projects you worked on that made you proud. Whenever you are enthusiastic about something, it is much easier to talk about it. It's good to be prepared for potential job interview questions by short-listing your finest accomplishments.

Evaluate your job over the past twelve months

✖ Have your skills improved? If so, how?

✖ Have you had new opportunities?

✖ Have you had new experiences?

✖ Have you worked towards your career goals? Which ones?

✖ What career goals have you achieved in the last twelve months?

✖ Have you been passed over for advancement? Why do you think it happened?

After you have completed the above exercise, give yourself an hour to draft one paragraph on each of the following topics:

✖ what I learned in my job

✖ what I achieved at my job

✖ what skills I have to offer a new employer

What do you want from a new position?

Use the work experiences you have had to date to continue to adapt and refine your goals and preferences. It's as important to know the things you don't like as the things you are looking for. Each job allows you to experience different management styles, working environments, responsibilities and challenges, and your next position should be a continued advancement towards realizing your work-related and financial goals.

Consider some of the following when determining your next best move.

✖ big company vs. small
✖ flexible hours
✖ benefits package
✖ training opportunities
✖ same job responsibilities/different company
✖ different responsibilities/same company
✖ salary
✖ promotion
✖ Different city/country
✖ specific company you want to work for

When you have determined what is important to you, take an hour to write a one-paragraph description of what you want from your next job.

Prepare your CV

Using the paragraphs you have written in the above exercise put together your CV. I am not an expert in CV writing, although as an employer I can tell you what made me decide to meet one candidate rather than another.

✖ **Keep it short.** I am a one-page person myself, but it depends on your profession and the length and breadth of your work experience. Keep it concise and accurate, but as brief as possible.

✖ **Keep it simple.** Don't go in for coloured inks or fancy typefaces. Black printing on a nice white or off-white heavy paper is stylish, not fussy and, most important, easy to read.

✖ **Write a covering letter.** Use your letter to show your enthusiasm for the position and very briefly, why you think you are right for the job. Be sure to research the correct person to send it to.

✖ **Pay attention to detail.** Double-check your spelling and grammar before sending anything off. I would never hire someone who doesn't have the sense to get it perfect to begin with. It's all in the detail for me.

✖ **Make it easy.** Provide a list of referees with contact details including phone, e-mail and address. Be sure to check with them first to see if they are around and willing to do it.

Network outside the company

Keep your eyes and ears open for all opportunities you may find interesting. Let your friends, family and professional contacts outside your office know you want to make a move.

interviews

If you are trying to squeeze interviews in while still working at your job, try not to put yourself under too much time pressure. Try to schedule an interview at the end of the day, after work if possible, so you don't feel rushed and worried. If you have many interviews, it's best to take a few days off work and try to schedule them together. If you know you are going to be late or can't make an appointment, give as much notice as possible and reschedule immediately so as not to miss the opportunity.

Do your homework

The Internet gives you the most amazing wealth of knowledge at your fingertips in a second. There is no excuse not to fully research the business and clients of the companies you may be interested in working for. The more effort you put into knowing about their business, the easier it will be for you to define the role you would like to play in their company. It's a great blending of egos!

Find out:

* how the company is doing financially
* how many people it employs
* who is in charge
* how it differs from its competitors
* where the offices are located
* if you know anyone who works there

Be prepared with questions you want to ask and remember the interviewing process goes both ways.

* What does the job entail?
* Is this a newly created position or a replacement post?
* Who will you be reporting to?
* How big is the team?
* What's the office like?
* Are there opportunities for advancement?
* Are there training programmes you can benefit from?
* What are the benefits?

✖ When does the position start?

✖ What is the salary?

Dress the part

Appearance plays an enormous part, stated or not, in employment decisions. Check out the office before the interview and look at the standards of dress. Stay away from excesses – perfume/aftershave, jewellery, make-up – and be certain your clothing is clean, fits well and is business like.

Show respect

Always be a few minutes early but definitely on time for any potential employer. Accept they may be running late and take the opportunity to review your notes and get psyched-up for the interview.

Turn off all mobile devices before you enter their office and give the interviewer your undivided attention. Never, ever interrupt. Use your eyes to communicate your interest in what they are saying, even if you jot down a few notes.

Always answer questions truthfully with a positive spin. If part of your reason for leaving your last job was to escape from an unhappy environment, don't be tempted in a weak moment to tattle about previous employers. Always define your reasons for leaving within the framework of achieving your goals.

Always send a follow-up thank-you note – whether you get the job or not. Good manners stick in the mind and as an employer I would always save a good CV for another occasion – perhaps with a different position in mind.

Never be too proud to work at something, even if it is beneath your qualifications

If the job market is tough and you can't find the ideal job, you can always take on temporary work to tide you over. If you are unemployed for a long time, aside from the financial ramifications, it can destroy your confidence, making it even more difficult to find the right job.

Look for work at something you enjoy, even if it's not your chosen profession. If you love fashion, music, books, computing, gardening, dogs or whatever, think about ways to utilize your skills and passions. You could make some money, gain time to continue the job search and use the experience to prove to a future employer your strength, determination and entrepreneurial nature. Who knows, you might just change your goals.

when you make the break

Give ample notice

As difficult as it may be to keep things quiet, it's best practice to tell your supervisor you are leaving before your colleagues. Timing plays a big part in how nervous you feel about the experience and the more people who know, the more pressure you feel under to resign. Choose the time when you feel comfortable, not at the insistence of others, and always do it face to face, in private, rather than just submitting your decision in writing.

Know your contractual obligations for giving notice and be prepared to work out that time in a professional manner. Make sure your boss knows how eager you are to cooperate in assuring a smooth transition and that you are willing to train someone in your role. Within the time frame of your notice period, work at tying up all loose ends and completing projects. Make notes explaining anything complicated. Leave your files organized and your office clean and tidy, with contact details where you can be reached should problems arise.

If for any reason your company wants you to leave prior to the notice period, be sure to discuss all compensation due to you, including bonuses, holiday pay and pension-scheme details. Let your supervisor announce your departure before discussing it with colleagues.

Always leave graciously

As tempting as it may be to speak your mind if you feel·negatively about your work, it won't gain you a thing. You will be holding on to anger and bitterness that will cloud your judgement when you could as easily choose to look at the benefits you have gained as a result of your positive experiences and happily move on.

The best way to leave to ensure good will and good references is to take the high road. Always explain the growth reasons for your decision to leave – it's much easier for the boss to swallow and you will be remembered in a favourable light. Thank your boss for all the opportunities and things you learned, whether you learned them as a result of your boss or not, and wish the company continued success when you depart.

Never bad-mouth the company to colleagues staying behind or to future employers and colleagues. No one likes a snitch, even if the tales you tell are true. Focus on the positive experiences – friends and accomplishments.

conclusion: what's next?

If you have ever tried to break a bad habit in the past, you know how difficult it can be. Each day you succeed at staying on course will help you further strengthen your resolve and enable you to accomplish your goals. You may still have challenges to face and on occasion you may even take a few steps backward and lapse into your old habits, but all is never lost. Sticking to difficult challenges brings the greatest rewards.

Your desire to work more efficiently is all it takes to begin the process. Implementing the strategies throughout this book will help you develop a realistic and manageable game plan to put in place on a daily basis and will bring great improvements to the quality of your working environment and your sense of achievement at the end of most days. There will always be the occasional hiccup, but take comfort in the knowledge that tomorrow is another day.

All habits over time – the good and the bad – become so routine that it is easy to go through the motions but fail to really take the time to think about what you are doing. To keep your newly acquired positive habits working for you, it is essential you assess continuously how you are getting on. At the beginning of each day, spend a few quiet minutes thinking about the easiest and best methods to achieve your to-do list and at the end of the day see how well you have done. By examining your work habits daily, you can fine-tune them to mesh with your own personal style and keep things on track. You will also avoid allowing things to build up into bigger problems.

Staying alert and aware of your weak spots can help you overcome them. The things you dislike doing the most are the things you need to learn to tackle first thing each day. Getting them off your mind is liberating and you will find that, in time, they will be less difficult to face. You just need to get a few successes under your belt to build up your confidence.

You will have failed at some of your goals and it is easy to get discouraged by that experience. Don't beat yourself up – you must know by now that it's impossible to be perfect. If you fail, implement a plan the next day and start again. You learn from cumulative experience and no matter how many times you have to try to get it right, if you really want to feel a true sense of accomplishment, master something that is difficult for you to do.

The only way to stay on the straight and narrow is to remind yourself daily of the reasons you began this process in the first place. Looking at the desired outcome is always the best incentive. Keep a list next to your computer of the three most meaningful reasons why you want to change your work habits and each day see how far you have come towards achieving them. Awareness of your actions is the key to continued success.

The knock-on effects of developing better work habits are enormous. When you feel satisfaction with your job at the end of the day, you can leave your work behind and enjoy your personal time. The more time you have to allow your body to be fully nourished and relaxed, the more refreshed you will feel at your job the following day. Good work habits ensure you get the balance right. Think about what changes your new work habits have had on your personal life.

Do a monthly review. Look at your office and see how well you are doing at maintaining a harmonious workspace. If you have fallen off the wagon, take immediate steps to rectify the situation. Action feels good. Look at the areas that have been a problem in the past and see what measurable progress you have made. Work on the things that are still not quite right by using your creativity to think of all the ways you have available to sort it out and try each and every idea until you find the one that works for you.

I hope that in the process of working through the great office detox you have made great strides towards developing a better working style and attitude. Be sure to reward yourself for all the effort you have made and share your success with the people who are important in your life. When good behaviour is reinforced with pleasant experiences, it helps you stick to your plans.

To keep the momentum going, push yourself to stay challenged and interested in your job. The desire to advance your career and learn new things is a great catalyst to keep you working at peak performance. Never forget that you are working towards something bigger – the dreams that your hard work will help you to achieve over time.

I wish you much success!

acknowledgements

I would like to thank the following people for their invaluable contributions to *The Great Office Detox*: Kate Adams, Liz Davis and everyone at Healthy Penguin for their enthusiasm and dedication to this project. Liz Chambers, Hugh Gilbert, George Gordon, Luca Gori, Karen Widermann and Joannna Kuhne for participating in an office detox. Celia Worster, Susie Worster, Sara Woodford, Rupert Burrows, Caroline Frazer, Tom Kerr, Matt Malaquias, Alison Walter, Jerry Walter, Emma Walter, Pattie Barron, Linda Sobotka, Sam Loggie and Kathryn Lloyd for helping me with research on work habits. Ann, Tibye, Sarina, Karen, Nina, Sergio, Jane – my great support network of buddies who are always there to add an opinion and to help me work things out. Carlos Isidio for looking after my dogs so well when I was too busy to take them for lovely walks in the park.

dawna walter
DE-JUNK YOUR MIND

'I have a really simple view of life. We're here for a good time, not a long time, so make every minute count. Like the physical clutter in your home, mental clutter slowly creeps up over the years without your even noticing. You can't rewrite history, but boy oh boy, you can start a new chapter today.'

On the hit TV programme *The Life Laundry*, Dawna Walter showed you how to de-clutter your house. Just like physical clutter, we all have mental baggage too, some of which needs to go in the crusher:

✖ old attitudes and beliefs
✖ negative behaviour patterns
✖ parental baggage
✖ relationships that have no positive impact on your life
✖ fear of change

De-Junk Your Mind is packed with practical exercises and a big dose of Dawna's tough love – it's time to take the plunge and change life for the better … now! The purpose of this book is to help you let go of the past and achieve your goals. Above all, it is a practical book structuring a game plan to boost your confidence and help you to be happier in all that you do.

L i v e   m o r e